INTO THE FIRE

I devoured this book in one sitting! Believers who are hungry
to see the power of God released in their lives need only
read this 21st-century addendum to the book of Acts.
Take courage, Church! Jesus is alive and moving in our midst.

JOSEPH GARLINGTON, SR.

SENIOR PASTOR, COVENANT CHURCH OF PITTSBURGH
PITTSBURGH, PENNSYLVANIA

Transparent and *radical* are two words that describe this
hard-hitting book by Ché Ahn. With a prophetic glint,
he chronicles the Holy Spirit's ruthless call upon his life to
raise up an apostolic stream of renewal and revival to touch
the ends of the earth. As you read, may your appetite be
whetted with a holy desire for more of the Lord!

JIM W. GOLL

FOUNDER OF MINISTRY TO THE NATIONS
ANTIOCH, TENNESSEE
AUTHOR OF *THE LOST ART OF INTERCESSION* AND
ENCOUNTERS WITH A SUPERNATURAL GOD

Ché Ahn's passion for the lost is the motivation which
compels his quest for revival. This man is no "sensation seeker,"
but is a solid, trustworthy spiritual leader. His vision and
vitality in pursuing God's grace upon the city of
Los Angeles makes him a joy to partner with in
pastoral fellowship and mission.

JACK W. HAYFORD

SENIOR PASTOR, THE CHURCH ON THE WAY
VAN NUYS, CALIFORNIA

INTO THE FIRE

Into the Fire makes a powerful impact.
Ché Ahn has opened his heart to us, and I believe this
extremely transparent book will be used to bring great personal
renewal to those who read it. I highly recommend it.

CINDY JACOBS

COFOUNDER, GENERALS OF INTERCESSION
COLORADO SPRINGS, COLORADO

Into the Fire is a spiritual bonanza for pastors
who are anxious for God to visit their churches. Ché Ahn
takes the whole subject of renewal and revival out of the
ethereal and places it into a practical, yet spiritual, context that
will speak to every church leader and layman. An excellent book.

RALPH MAHONEY

DIRECTOR, WORLD MISSIONARY ASSISTANCE PLAN
BURBANK, CALIFORNIA

This book is from a man who has followed hard after God to
see Him move in his church in astonishing ways. What Ché Ahn
has done is almost unthinkable for a successful man of his culture
and heritage. He has willingly bared his own weaknesses and
failures to pass on to us what he has learned about the ways of
God in revival. In a culture characterized by so much shallow
syncretism and easy, media-weary dismissal of conviction, passion
and commitment, Jesus the Lord is moving again to touch a new
generation with power, wonder and purity. This book is both a
record and a challenge to touch again the hem of His garment
for your own life and ministry.

WINKIE PRATNEY

AUTHOR, MISSIONARY AND EVANGELIST
LINDALE, TEXAS

INTO THE FIRE

Having known Ché Ahn as a friend and fellow leader for more
than 22 years, I enthusiastically commend this book to believers
everywhere. You'll identify with his struggles and be challenged
by his journey from renewal to revival. Make his quest your
own and you'll never be the same!

LARRY TOMCZAK

FACULTY, BROWNSVILLE REVIVAL SCHOOL OF MINISTRY
ACWORTH, GEORGIA

For years I have watched the Holy Spirit at work
in the lives of Ché Ahn and Harvest Rock Church.
In *Into the Fire*, Ahn not only tells this awesome story,
but he skillfully draws from it unchanging principles
you can apply in order to experience more
fruit in your life and ministry.

C. PETER WAGNER

PROFESSOR, FULLER THEOLOGICAL SEMINARY
AUTHOR AND EDITOR OF *THE RISING REVIVAL*
COLORADO SPRINGS, COLORADO

Ché Ahn has written an absorbing account of an ongoing miracle
of renewal, growth, discovery, revival and world outreach—
the tapestry of God's leading.

RALPH D. WINTER

GENERAL DIRECTOR, FRONTIER MISSION FELLOWSHIP
PASADENA, CALIFORNIA

INTO THE FIRE

HOW YOU CAN ENTER RENEWAL AND CATCH GOD'S HOLY FIRE

CHÉ AHN

Renew

A Division of Gospel Light
Ventura, California, U.S.A.

Published by Renew Books
A Division of Gospel Light
Ventura, California, U.S.A.
Printed in U.S.A.

Renew Books is a ministry of Gospel Light, an evangelical Christian publisher dedicated to serving the local church. We believe God's vision for Gospel Light is to provide church leaders with biblical, user-friendly materials that will help them evangelize, disciple and minister to children, youth and families.

It is our prayer that this Renew book will help you discover biblical truth for your own life and help you meet the needs of others. May God richly bless you.

For a free catalog of resources from Renew Books/Gospel Light please contact your Christian supplier or call 1-800-4-GOSPEL.

Cover Design by Barbara LeVan Fisher
Interior Design by Britt Rocchio
Edited by Virginia Woodard

Library of Congress Cataloging-in-Publication Data
Ahn, Ché, 1956-
    Into the fire / Ché Ahn.
        p. cm.
    Includes bibliographical references.
    ISBN 0-8307-2149-5 (trade paper)
    1. Church renewal—California—Case studies. 2. Evangelistic work. 3. Ahn, Ché, 1956-   . I.
Title.
    BV600.2.A24 1998   98-23589
    269—dc21   CIP

1 2 3 4 5 6 7 8 9 10 11 12 13 14 15 16 17 18 / 05 04 03 02 01 00 99 98

Rights for publishing this book in other languages are contracted by Gospel Literature International (GLINT). GLINT also provides technical help for the adaptation, translation and publishing of Bible study resources and books in scores of languages worldwide. For further information, contact GLINT, P.O. Box 4060, Ontario, CA 91761-1003, U.S.A., or the publisher.

To my wonderful wife, Sue,

and my four special children,

Gabriel, Grace, Joy and Mary.

CONTENTS

—■—

FOREWORD

We are in the midst of a historic visitation of the Holy Spirit! On January 20, 1994, our church exploded with a touch from God, and since then we have seen Him extend that touch of His wonderful Spirit to the nations of the world. Many people are calling this move of the Spirit "renewal," while others are calling it "revival." Regardless of how we label this awesome move of God, people's hearts have been captivated. They continue to visit us here in Toronto, and in many places such as Pasadena, California, because they are hungry for more of Him. Thousands have testified about dynamic change and blessing in their lives.

My dear friend Ché Ahn writes in a very transparent way about his experience with renewal. He shares how renewal has changed his life, his ministry and even his marriage. He has seen some amazing things since 1994, and his testimonies will inspire and encourage you. Yet even though we are in revival to a measure, Ché, I and others are longing and believing for more. We desire to see increased salvations, more healing and a far greater advancement for the kingdom of God to the point of significant social change in our society. Ché brings valuable insight into how it can happen.

I have had the privilege of visiting hundreds of churches around the world that are welcoming the "river." Of the many Christian leaders I now know, I believe that Ché has truly pastored the renewal well. His church has grown significantly since its inception in 1994 and is a unique model of how God is creating "new wineskins" for this outpouring.

Pastors in particular will be able to relate to this book because Ché shares not only the successes of his calling, but also his failures and disappointments during his years of pastoral ministry. He weaves into this book's pages biblical principles that will enable leaders to effectively pastor this move of God and to truly experience both renewal and growth.

Any individual who is simply hungry for more of God will also find sustenance in these chapters, as will any person who is struggling in a marriage or relationship with other loved ones. Ché does an incredible job of sharing the transforming reconciliation that happened to him in his relationship both with his father and his own wife. The healing principles he imparts as received from John and Paula Sandford have not only freed and encouraged thousands of believers around the world, but changed my own relationship with my wife, Carol, as well.

Vast numbers of new books speak about revival, many of which are noteworthy. Yet this book, in my opinion, is one of the most important because Ché is not writing out of theory as a theologian or an academician, even though he is both of these, but as one who has truly experienced and is experiencing an unusual move of the Holy Spirit. I believe that Ché's book is a further catalyst to spread the flames of revival around the world.

John Arnott, Senior Pastor
Toronto Airport Christian Fellowship
Toronto, Canada

Acknowledgments

Without sounding too spiritual, I want to thank my heavenly Father for the way He initiated and helped me write this book. It has been a miraculous and wonderful journey in and of itself.

Thank you, Sue, for loving me, standing by me, and your special help in writing the chapter about us. Thank you to my dear children, for always being supportive, and willing to share your lives unselfishly with others.

Thank you, Bessie Watson, my personal assistant, for your outstanding job of editing the manuscript, and Audrey Eckhardt, my faithful assistant, always ready and helpful in every way. Thank you, Cindy Jacobs, for giving me a word to write the book.

I will never forget how God orchestrated the events in Portland, Oregon, which led to Regal becoming my publisher. Thank you, Kyle Duncan and Bill Greig III, for believing in me and this book. Many thanks to Virginia Woodard and David Webb, editors of Regal and Renew books.

A special thanks to my father, Rev. Byung Kook Ahn, and my mother, Young Sook Ahn, for all you have given and spoken into my life and for your blessing on the chapter about us.

None of my life would be worth reading about without the many incredible men and women of God who have made such a foundational investment in me and my call in Christ through the years. You have mentored me as a peer, discipled me as a son and a brother, come and spoken at our conferences, and given life to Harvest Rock Church and the vision of God to which we are called. I am eternally grateful. I especially want to acknowledge my spiritual mentors Larry Tomczak, Winkie Pratney, Peter Wagner and Jack Hayford.

I most want to thank the wonderful members of Harvest Rock Church, as well as its pastors—Lou and Therese Engle, Rick and Pam Wright, Jeff and Joan Wright, Jim and Laura Johnson, Karl and Debbie Malouff, Carlos and Brenda Quintero, and Paul and Catherine Lee—because without you there would have been nothing to write about.

INTRODUCTION

This book is my simple offering to you of one man's journey through renewal...one that spawned a new church...a new movement...a new man...a renewed marriage...a new motive...and a consuming new passion for revival.

Historically, "renewal" and "revival" have been used as interchangeable terms. For the purposes of this book, however, I have chosen to define them differently.

I am using "renewal" to describe the sovereign refreshing God is bringing to His Church and those already a part of it. It is glorious, needed and welcomed. As John Arnott declares, "This move of the Spirit is first of all about a renewal and refreshing for Christians, finding out what a wonderful, loving Savior we have; second, it is about loving our neighbor-evangelism."[1]

"Revival," then, is the *continuum* of this wave as it sweeps over the community at large. When it hits, a great awakening occurs and an unusually large number of non-Christians are brought into the Kingdom in a relatively short time period. Everything changes. God becomes a central focus of the community. This then is what I am longing for. Revival with a capital *R*. A historic revival where a whole nation is changed.

Winkie Pratney summarized several scholars' excellent definitions of revival in his work *Revival: Its Principles and Personalities.*[2]

The revived church by many or few is moved to engage in evangelism, teaching and social action. (J. Edwin Orr)

A community saturated with God. (Duncan Campbell)

Revival must of necessity make an impact on the community, and this is one means by which we may distinguish it from the more usual operations of the Holy Spirit. (Arthur Wallis)

John Dawson points out that "community" now means those hundreds or thousands of miles away and/or linked by common vocation and communication.

MY PASSION FOR REVIVAL

As a young teen strung out on drugs and fully sated with the pleasures of partying, I found myself empty, aimless and lost. Then I came to know Jesus during a historic revival called the Jesus Movement.

Perhaps that is why I love revival so much and am passionate about envisioning another visitation that will once again sweep young people into His kingdom and truly change lives. More than just "church" or a set of rules to follow, I had a radical conversion experience with a living God and a relationship with Jesus that transformed every fiber of my being and the very reason I lived.

Many others besides me believe revival is once again imminent upon us. Most believe, as do I, that this revival will be greater than any previous revival in the entire history of the Church.

SIGNS OF REVIVAL

What are some of the signs of revival?

First, never before have there been such movements of prayer in the United States and around the globe as we are experiencing now. John Wesley once said, "Everything by prayer, and nothing without it." Prayer must precede any great revival, and it is now being put into place. Never before have so many organizations, so many denominations and so many networks given themselves to the purpose of prayer and to the purposes of praying together.

I agree with Dr. C. Peter Wagner's encouraging assessment: "We who are living today have the privilege of living in the midst of the greatest worldwide prayer movement that Christianity has ever known."[3]

Just consider: History was made when more than one million men from every race and background gathered in Washington, D.C., on October 4, 1997 to simply humble themselves in repentance and prayer. Thousands of prayer initiatives and ministry groups have emerged across the nation, facilitating conferences, convocations, schools of prayer and the like. People such as Dr. C. Peter Wagner of Global Harvest Ministries are doing a tremendous job equipping and mobilizing thousands to pray for revival and a worldwide harvest.

Further, the initiatives span the entire Body of Christ, including denominational believers and evangelicals such as Campus Crusade for Christ's Dr. Bill Bright. Dr. Bright is calling for two million believers to pray and fast for 40 days before the year 2000.[4] In my travels and in the copious networking materials I read, I have never before heard of or met so many people who are fasting and praying for revival.

Second, we are observing reconciliation and unification among members of the Body of Christ as never before. We are noticing individuals and ethnic groups forgive and unite, pastors and denominations and movements unify, and the spiritual climates of cities change. Thank God for Promise Keepers, as well as leaders such as John Dawson, Pastor Jack Hayford, Ed Silvoso, Cindy Jacobs and Ted Haggard who are bringing healing and reconciliation to the Body of Christ.

Third, we are now observing the beginning stages of the harvest. Many were thrilled when in the small city of Modesto,

California, 33,000 people came to Christ when the play "Heaven's Gates, Hell's Flames" was presented in 1995. Churches such as Willow Creek in Chicago and Saddleback Community in Saddleback, California, are exploding with conversion growth. In revival centers such as Brownsville Assembly of God in Pensacola, Florida, more than 100,000 have been saved in their protracted meetings since Father's Day, 1995. By the time this book is published, that statistic will be obsolete!

The fourth sign is that the Church at large has been experiencing unusual renewal since January 1994. The "Toronto Blessing," led by my good friends John and Carol Arnott, exploded upon the world, starting in Canada—and similar renewals are aflame in such countries as Argentina.

Filled with the tangible presence of God, a call to deep and intimate relationship with the Lord, and accompanied by signs, wonders, miracles and unmistakable personal visitation and refreshing, this renewal has spread like wildfire. From the last report I heard, more than two million people have visited Toronto, experienced renewal and brought the "renewal fire" back to churches around the world. I heard John Arnott say that this visitation has spread to every nation and every denomination in a very short time.

Although many have found this movement controversial, I have maintained it is either the biggest deception to hit the Church in the history of the Church, or it is the beginning of a great revival. I believe the latter to be true.

For me, this presence of renewal is the clearest sign revival is imminent. Why? Because I believe that often throughout history renewal precedes revival.

Using the book of Acts as our pattern, look at the chronology toward revival. In Acts 2, 120 believers were filled with the Holy Spirit and renewed in the Upper Room. Then, 3,000 unbelievers came to Christ as Peter preached on the Day of Pentecost.

Consider the history of revival in the United States. We observe a similar pattern. As I have talked to historians about the Azusa Street Revival that occurred in Los Angeles in 1906, they have told me few people were really converted, but amazing numbers of Christians came to receive the infilling of the Holy Spirit and other spiritual gifts such as speaking in tongues.

John Arnott says Azusa "was known for pastors and leaders who were powerfully touched by the Holy Spirit who then took the blessing home to their churches and started revivals locally. That is where the harvest came from."[5]

After that time in Azusa, we have observed the birth of the Pentecostal and charismatic movements and those entering the kingdom of God en masse through them. Indeed, the Pentecostals and charismatics are the fastest-growing movements in Christendom worldwide, and account for more than four-fifths of the world's Christians.[6]

Likewise, many "non-Pentecostal" Christians experienced the Holy Spirit in new ways during the charismatic renewal in the 1960s and 1970s. Following that renewal, the Jesus Movement revival swept millions of young people like me into the Kingdom.

I am firmly convinced that the revival toward which we are headed will dwarf anything in recent memory or the history books!

THE THRUST OF THIS BOOK

My personal journey into renewal and my quest for revival is the purpose of this book. My fervent prayer is to stir those of you who have already entered into the rivers of renewal to settle for nothing less than the flood waters of revival...and to encourage those of you who have never entered the stream to begin to excitedly take the plunge!

I will take you there chapter by chapter, offering helpful action tips at the end of each section.

Chapter 1 shares how I came to experience renewal, and how it revolutionized my life and my calling to ministry. Much more is available for each of us as the waters of revival rise (see Ezek. 47).

Chapter 2 relates the birthing of our new church—Harvest Rock—one of thousands God is establishing as catalysts and containers for the coming revival. I tell our story to encourage you and your church to prepare for the greatest harvest of all time.

Chapter 3 illuminates the importance of the prophetic ministry and the foundation of prophets (see Eph. 2:20) in this hour, and how we can best hear what the Spirit is saying to the Church.

Chapter 4 describes the apostolic network God has permitted us to establish, called Harvest International Ministries. It gives insight into many new networks, associations and movements God is birthing to retain the great harvest, as also occurred in past revivals.

Chapter 5 recounts faith-building testimonies of healings I have witnessed in this renewal. As in the book of Acts, I believe one of the outstanding characteristics of this revival will be physical healings. You will be greatly encouraged by these accounts of our loving Father's miraculous touch.

Chapter 6 takes you into a new dimension of "power evangelism" that is filled with the supernatural presence of God. Power evangelism moves us beyond "rote" witnessing to usher in a revelation of Jesus Christ that few can resist. This is vital for the coming harvest!

Chapter 7 describes our basis in prayer. This could have been the first chapter, for no renewal or revival ever happened without the church first praying. I share how the prayer we experienced changed from drudgery to fruitfulness, how God gave us a unique strategy for our city and the nations, and how He now has intercessors praying 24 hours a day!

Chapter 8 tells how God developed in me a heart for my city, and took me from a sectarian bias to a position of helping bring ethnic and racial reconciliation to Los Angeles.

Chapters 9 and 10 are in many ways what I consider to be the most important chapters in the book. As their texts unfold, you will notice how the most cherished bottom line of renewal for me has been changed relationships—first with God, then with my family and loved ones, and then with all those within my world.

Chapter 9 specifically imparts how the greatest reconciliation and renewal of all begins in the home. "He will turn the hearts of the fathers to their children, and the hearts of the children to their fathers" (Mal. 4:6). My personal journey of healing in my relationship with my dad has changed my ministry and my life.

Chapter 10 takes my story even more deeply into the personal change and growth in my life as a result of renewal in God's love. I share how the Lord dealt with me about my relationship with my wife, Sue, and how repentance and God's deep work gave us a new marriage. I pray that every believer, leader or pastoral couple who reads this chapter will be helped in their relationships. This coming harvest—and our personal joy and satisfaction in life—demands honest, healed individuals who will parent these new Christians and model loving family life.

My final chapter aspires to help us each move forward in our quest for revival. God is sovereign, and we cannot force His hand. I believe with all my heart we can, as we are urged in 2 Peter 3:12, look forward to "hastening the coming of the day of God" (NKJV) through our obedience. Revival is the Father's heart desire for a hurting world. I offer what I sense are some of God's most vital criteria for you and me to encourage His desire to come to pass.

Whether you are hungering for personal renewal or more actively desiring a historical revival, I pray this book will bless and enrich you...and contribute clearly to His purposes in your life.

Notes
1. John Arnott, *The Father's Blessing* (Lake Mary, Fla.: Creation House, 1995), p. 29.
2. Winkie Pratney, *Revival: Its Principles and Personalities* (Lafayette, La.: Huntington House Publishers, 1994), pp. 16, 17.

3. Alice Smith, *Beyond the Veil* (Ventura, Calif.: Renew Books, 1997), p. 11. From C. Peter Wagner's foreword.
4. Bill Bright, *The Coming Revival* (Orlando, Fla.: New Life Publications, 1995)
5. Arnott, *The Father's Blessing*, p. 219.
6. C. Peter Wagner, *Spiritual Power and Church Growth* (Lake Mary, Fla.: Strang Communications, 1986).

RENEWED

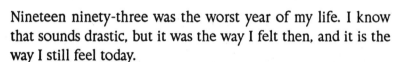

Nineteen ninety-three was the worst year of my life. I know that sounds drastic, but it was the way I felt then, and it is the way I still feel today.

After nine years of struggling as a pastor in Southern California, I had finally called it quits. I never thought things would turn out this way.

MY VIVID DREAM

Initially, I had a lot of faith and vision for a great church. After all, God had literally given me a vision of coming to Los Angeles. It was more of a dream than a vision, but a dream had never been so real to me. It seemed to be a summons from the throne room of God.

At four o'clock in the morning of the second day of September 1982, exactly three years from the date of my ordination, an African-American appeared to me in a dream and spoke these words: "The Lord wants you to come to Los Angeles and establish a church, for there will be a great harvest."

I awakened, experiencing waves of the Lord's presence coursing through my body. The captivating words and melody of a song we sang at church played again and again in my mind: *The time of revival is here.*

Immediately, I got down on my knees and began to pray.

Finally, I could wait no more. Around 5:30 A.M. I awakened my wife, Sue, and excitedly shared the dream with her. Immediately, she bore witness to all I had seen, and we began to pray spontaneously and rejoice in this new revelation.

Things were set into motion in our hearts beginning that day. Our plans seemed further ordained through more confirmations that followed. Just as Gideon asked the Lord for a sign to show clearly that He was with him, so Sue and I threw out a fleece to the Lord.

We prayed that my best friend and pastor at the time, Larry Tomczak, would take the initiative to ask me if I wanted to plant a church, as I was also a member of his pastoral team. That would serve as my cue to share all that God had put into my heart about going to Los Angeles.

Confirmation from My Pastor and the Pastoral Team

Six months after my dream, Larry asked me if I wanted to go out for lunch. I knew in my heart this was the day Larry would ask me if I wanted to plant a church. I can't really tell you how I knew; I just knew. In the same way I was confident my earlier dream had been of the Lord, I knew He would also confirm it.

Soon we were seated at lunch and I heard Larry say to me, "Ché, I'm sensing that we are too top heavy with pastors in our church. I feel that we should send you out to plant a church. Do you have any desire to plant a church? If so, where?" he asked.

I could barely contain myself. "I thought you would never ask!" I exclaimed. I told him everything...the dream, the fleece, the call to Los Angeles.

"Los Angeles?" he queried incredulously. "I was thinking a little bit closer to home, like northern Virginia or something," he added.

"Larry, I really believe this is of God," I affirmed. He seemed open to the idea, and suggested I share it with our fellow pastors at our next meeting together to find out what they thought.

As I shared, each of the pastors was similarly open to what I felt God was leading me to do. As a safeguard, they encouraged me to take some additional time to seek God and pray for further confirmation.

Confirmation from TV

My wife and I decided to get away and spend three days together in prayer and fasting to be sure about what we were hearing. We borrowed my uncle's condominium in Ocean City, Maryland—a popular beach resort a few hours away on the Atlantic Ocean. As we entered the condo, we set down our bags, knelt on the floor and asked God to please give us the confirmation we needed regarding a move to Los Angeles.

At that moment, in a passing flash, I had an impression that we were to turn on the television, and that the "700 Club" would be aired on TV. I said to Sue, almost jokingly, "Honey, let's turn on the TV and see if Pat Robertson is on. Maybe he'll have a word of knowledge for us."

It wasn't like me to say something like that. In the natural scheme of things, it made even less sense. What were the odds that his show aired in Ocean City, much less at this time of day? We didn't have a program schedule, and I wasn't sure the condo had a working TV, as we were visiting during the off season.

The condo did have a television set, however, and it did work, and as I began to flip the channels, sure enough, the "700 Club" was showing! I saw Ben Kinchlow and Pat Robertson praying over a stack of letters. Then they started to give words of knowledge, or specific impressions they were sensing God supernaturally saying (see 1 Cor. 12:8) concerning various physical conditions the Lord was healing.

Then, Pat paused and gave this word of knowledge: "There is a pastor who is asking God for a confirmation about planting a church. The Lord says that this is of Him. And if you go out in unity and in harmony, the Lord will give you great success."

I couldn't believe what I was hearing. I shouted to Sue, "This is the confirmation we're looking for!" She and I were so ecstatic that we began to give praise to God and dance around the condo. Incredible!

Then I had another idea. Perhaps the same "700 Club" show would air again later in the day on that same channel, as I knew it did at home. If so, I could tape-record that word of knowledge and play it later for my fellow pastors!

We kept the channel on all that afternoon and evening. Sure enough, the program played again that evening, and we were ready, holding the portable tape recorder in our hands. The recording turned out perfectly. Grateful and confident that God had indeed answered our prayers for confirmation, instead of fasting for three days, we were able to celebrate and had a wonderful minivacation.

The following Tuesday when I met with the other pastors, I shared exactly what had happened and played the tape. As one brother said, "I sense the presence of the Holy Spirit came in during the playing of the recording. The idea of Ché and Sue going to Los Angeles is of the Lord." Having received the pastors' confirmation and blessing, we knew it would only be a matter of time before we would be sent to Los Angeles.

SENT TO PASADENA

Following a time of careful preparation and transition, my family and three other couples and a few singles were sent from Maryland to plant a new church in Pasadena, California, just on the outskirts of Los Angeles.

At 28 years old, I was ready to single-handedly bring another Azusa Street Revival[1] to Los Angeles—or so I thought. That is when the trials began. That is when God started to break me.

Many times I found myself lying prostrate on the floor and crying. Instead of asking for the God of Elijah, I wondered if I would ever see the "God of Revival."

My friends (and later to become fellow pastors) Lou Engle,

David Warnick and I did everything we knew to fulfill the vision. No doubt that was part of the problem.

We held early morning prayer meetings together for years. For the most part, it was a real challenge for me to wake up early. I am more of a night owl than an early-morning person. Although we had some seasons of outstanding prayer when 40 or 50 people packed the prayer room and we knew God was in our presence, for the most part, we were "paying the price" and wondering if our prayers were being heard.

███

WHEN A BROTHER QUIPPED, "THE '80S
WERE FROM HADES," THAT ABOUT
SUMMARIZED MY DECADE.

On other fronts, we did everything possible to evangelize during that decade. We did open-air preaching at California State of Los Angeles. We went door-to-door witnessing. We performed street theater. We went into the ghettos. We held special meetings. We brought in special speakers, but we saw little fruit.

Eventually, the church started to grow, and God started to add some wonderful people...but it was a far cry from revival.

SHAKEN BY CIRCUMSTANCES

When a brother quipped, "The '80s were from Hades," that about summarized my decade. Given the scandals among television evangelists, it was not a fun time to be in the ministry. My own struggles made it doubly difficult. When anyone asked me what I did for a living, I was tempted to say "sales," or even "insurance"—*anything* but ministry!

Then, as I was hoping for the end of a bad decade, and the beginning of a better decade, the bottom fell out completely.

The first cross-cultural church plant, sponsored by the larger ministry team of which I was a part, blew up in our faces.

Without rehashing all the details, I was primarily responsible for what had happened with our overseas efforts. The end result was that missions were placed on an indefinite hold in our church and in the organization as a whole.

Because our church had sent the missionaries, and because we had built our church on a mission vision, many of our church members left. This change in direction left them disillusioned with both our local body and the larger church-planting ministry. More than 100 people left within a six-month period.

I often wished I were among them, but the Lord would not release me. Although much good fruit did come from this ministry, in no way can I describe the devastation in my heart as the vision I had for the world seemed to disappear.

Eventually, a leadership change took place in the movement we were part of, and the new leader made it clear to me that we were no longer going to plant churches in Asia or anywhere else except the United States and Mexico.

Ever since I was a young believer, I had an intense burden for missions and for internationals, and it fueled the majority of my pursuit of God and all to which I set my hand. The death of that vision caused me to begin to spiritually die.

Words fail to describe the passion and like-hearted commitment we had held together to see the Kingdom birthed around the world, and now the emptiness I felt inside knowing that it would never be a reality.

Somehow I made it to 1993. By January, however, Sue and I knew we were to resign as pastors and leave both our church and the larger organization. It was the hardest decision we ever made in our lives.

We had been with the founders of our movement for 19 years. It meant leaving our friends with whom we had built our closest relationships and raised our children, including our best friends Larry and Doris Tomczak. My sister and my relatives were still involved with the mother church in Maryland.

A "Word" from the Lord

We knew God had spoken clearly to us. One of the ways He confirmed our move was through Cindy Jacobs, a leader and prophetess in the Body of Christ. The Lord woke her up and spoke to her to intercede for us. Then God gave her a prophetic word for us—or a specific directive inspired by the Holy Spirit (see Acts 13:1-3; 21:10,11; 1 Cor. 14:1).

Cindy had never called us before. In fact, she had to call a friend to find our phone number. She lived three states away and had no idea what was going on with us. No one had been told because we were waiting on the Lord for the timing and the proper way to share the changes.

Cindy called and ministered a word to us that we would be leaving our church and our movement, but it would not be until 1994. She also said that 1993 would be the hardest year of our lives. Emotions flooded through me, along with mixed feelings about receiving such a difficult word.

It was somewhat comforting to know that my wife and I had heard a word from God about this most difficult decision, and that it was confirmed by a well-known and respected prophetess. The disconcerting part was facing the hardship we would encounter. True to the word, the "spaghetti soon hit the fan."

When I shared the decision with my fellow pastors and leaders of the movement, they were angry and disappointed. At stake were other issues of doctrine and philosophy of ministry I would rather not expound upon, but, ultimately, I no longer had faith to continue in a movement that had lost the original vision for world missions.

I was torn. I loved the people of the church, but how could I continue in a movement with which I no longer agreed? The Bible says in Amos 3:3, "Do two walk together unless that have agreed to do so?" It was the hardest decision Sue and I have ever made in our Christian lives. It felt like jumping out of a plane without a parachute, but I knew the Lord would be my confidant and guide. My desires were to obey His leading and try to make the transition as painless for the church as possible.

A Difficult Transition Period

The leaders accepted my resignation as senior pastor, but asked me to stay for a one-year transition period. I agreed. I stepped down as senior pastor and became a staff evangelist. A pastor I

■

NINETEEN NINETY-THREE REMAINS THE WORST
YEAR OF MY LIFE. I DIDN'T REALIZE IT THEN,
BUT GOD WAS BREAKING ME AND PREPARING
ME FOR 1994, THE YEAR GOD WOULD BEGIN TO
FULFILL THE DREAM OF THE PROMISED REVIVAL.

had trained became the new senior pastor. Now the young man to whom I was a pastor while he was in seminary became my new pastor and my boss. My salary was drastically reduced and, to say the least, so was my pride. The real pain I was facing, though, was deep confusion and personal disillusionment.

In all candor, I had no idea what was coming next. Although I knew God was asking me to resign and for Sue and me soon to leave the church we had planted, nothing else was clear. All I wanted to do was to sell our home and leave California...and be anywhere but Los Angeles.

Suddenly I found myself sinking into a deep depression. I was rarely depressed, but I knew I was hurting. The roof felt as if it were caving in on me. My neck was wrenched in pain, and my body felt heavy and old under the stress. My family and I were suffering financially from the drastic salary cut. Without much success, I was trying to make up the difference in income by doing itinerant work. It was a devastating and long six months.

We finally borrowed on the equity of our home to pay our bills. All the while, we were feeling rejected by our closest friends and they felt rejected by us because we desired to leave our church and the movement. To top it off, I was mad at God for bringing us to California and not fulfilling the dream He had supernaturally given me.

I wanted to quit the ministry, move to a ranch and train a watchdog to bite anyone who was carrying a Bible. Not really, but I felt close to that. Anything I could say at this point really couldn't do justice to what I experienced that year. It was a year I wouldn't wish on anyone. That is why 1993 remains the worst year of my life.

I didn't realize it then, but God was breaking me and preparing me for 1994, the year God would begin to fulfill the dream of the promised revival.

HOLY LAUGHTER

In January 1994, Toronto, Canada, experienced an awakening that would be heard around the world. A major outpouring, or visitation of the Holy Spirit, had begun.[2] What many do not realize is at the very same time, this same kind of renewal hit the Anaheim Vineyard Christian Fellowship in California.

It began on a Sunday night as the church was sending out the youth for a short-term mission trip. The Holy Spirit fell on the kids with unusually strong manifestations. Manifestations—various physical and emotional expressions that happen when a person encounters the raw supernatural power of God—often include laughing, crying, shaking, jerking or unusual sounds (see Jer. 23:9; Rom. 8:26; Rev. 1:17). Such expressions have been common in visitations of God throughout history.[3]

The next week, the Vineyard held its annual conference. That particular year the conference theme was "healing," featuring guest speakers Francis McNutt and Mahesh Chavda, two evangelists well known for their healing gifts. The renewal spilled over into the conference in a powerful way.

Lou Engle and I had registered for the conference and had no clue that a fresh revival was beginning in the Vineyard movement. That quickly changed the first day of the conference as we saw with our own eyes the Holy Spirit falling on people, producing unusual manifestations of laughter, shaking and other loud cries and noises.

Initially, I was cynical about what was occurring. I had read about Rodney Howard Brown and "holy laughter" in *Charisma* magazine, but had never experienced it. I thought the people were laughing through mass suggestion and hysteria and not through a genuine move of the Holy Spirit. One day during the conference, however, people seated in separate sections of the auditorium all laughed at one time as the Holy Spirit swept through the hall like a fresh wind.

My friend Lou poked me with his elbow and excitedly yelled, "It's coming toward us! It's coming toward us!"

I remember saying, "Well, I'm not going to laugh." When the Holy Spirit hit our section, though, I felt myself becoming inebriated. I could not stop laughing. It lasted at least 20 minutes. Everything was funny...even though no one was saying anything funny.

A bald man was sitting in front of me, and for whatever reason, his bald head looked funny to me. So I leaned over and began to massage his head. He didn't care; he was laughing, too. It was a wonderful, refreshing experience that seemed to invigorate every part of my being. I didn't notice until later that my depression was gone!

How God moved on me surprised me as much as it must have John Arnott in Toronto, where it all began. As he puts it, "We had been praying for God to move, and our assumption was that we would see more people saved and healed, along with the excitement that these would generate. It never occurred to us that God would throw a massive party where people would laugh, roll, cry, and become so empowered that emotional hurts from childhood were just lifted off of them. The phenomena may be strange, but the fruit this is producing is extremely good."[4]

The result of this experience was immediate fruit in my life! I was excited about ministry again. More important, I was once again in love with Jesus. I felt His presence, and I knew something incredible had happened in my life. Yet it was only the beginning of a life-changing week.

EMPOWERED BY THE SPIRIT

The next day, Mahesh Chavda spoke. He shared a dream he had dreamed the night before. He dreamt that a pastor had brought two loaves of bread to the conference. Then he shared his interpretation of the dream: The pastor represented all the pastors at the conference.

At least 500 out of 4,000 attendees were pastors. The bread represented the healing anointing. He made references to the Syrophoenician woman who begged Jesus to come and heal her daughter. Jesus replied that it was not good to give the children's bread (the healing) to the dogs (Gentiles) (see Matt. 15:26).

37

She responded that even dogs can eat the crumbs left over by the children. Noticing her faith, Jesus pronounced that her daughter was healed (see Mark 7:24-30). Mahesh Chavda's point was that pastors were to take back to their home churches the healing anointing that was being imparted.

As Mahesh was sharing his dream, I was jumping out of my seat. As I left home in the morning to go to the conference, my wife handed me two loaves of homemade raisin bread to take with me. I had never brought bread to a conference before, or since!

Sue had simply been toying with a bread maker I had given her for Christmas and thought I might enjoy taking some loaves to eat and to share. When Mahesh began talking about a pastor who had brought bread that day, I wondered if the dream could be about me. I was trembling inside, feeling anticipation and wonder.

As the session closed, Mahesh began to pray for people individually in a time of personal ministry. I made my way forward through the crowd to talk with him. As our eyes met, I said, "Mahesh, you don't know me, but I am a pastor, and my wife gave me two loaves of bread to bring to this conference."

His eyes widened and he said, "You stay here!" He quickly went to the platform and grabbed a mike and said, "Ladies and gentlemen, may I have your attention!" A hush fell over the audience. "There is a pastor here who brought two loaves of bread, just like I explained in my dream. We are going to pray for him!"

He walked up to me and placed his hands on my head. All I can remember is that I went flying backward and landed on my back, shaking violently. That was the first time I had really been "slain in the Spirit"—or had the power of God cause me to fall to the floor (see John 18:1-6).

(Yes, I had gone down before when other leaders had prayed for me; but I have to admit I never felt anything. It was what I call "courtesy falls." You fall down even if you don't feel anything so as not to embarrass the minister or people who seem to expect it.)

This time it was different. I had never before experienced so much power through the laying on of hands. I used to be irritated with people in the Vineyard who would shake while praying—and now I was shaking uncontrollably! What is more amazing is that I have been shaking ever since that day!

Whenever I worship or sense the presence of the Holy Spirit, my hands shake, sometimes more violently than other times. I don't fully understand these phenomenons or manifestations, but it makes sense to me that if you touch raw electricity, your body reacts. If you touch the power of God, it should not be a shock that you react physically. When the supernatural meets the natural, a response will result!

Although my purpose is not to give an apologetic for the manifestations at the renewal, I would simply like to share what happened to me. I wasn't seeking to shake, but I did; and I have been shaking ever since.[5]

A Powerful Impartation Resulted

I also received a powerful impartation (see 1 Tim. 4:14; 2 Tim. 1:6) at the time Mahesh prayed for me, which I didn't realize until the following week.

Lou Engle and I were asked to participate in a youth conference the following week in Pasadena. Throughout the youth
conference, the Holy Spirit fell upon the young people just as
we had seen at the healing conference the previous week.

Kids shook and fell under the power of the Holy Spirit. I
then realized that Lou and I had received something very trans-
ferable and wonderfully contagious. Yet what really shocked
me took place in a seminar I held at the conference.

After I spoke, a young girl around 13 years old came to me
and said, "Could you please pray for my left eye? I am completely blind in that eye. I was at a carnival as a little girl and a
metal object flew into my eye and severely damaged it. I have
had three eye surgeries and nothing has helped. I am completely blind in that eye."

As she was explaining her situation to me, I could feel what
little faith I had begin to ooze out of me. I honestly had no
faith for her to be healed. I had prayed before for several people who had been blind, and none of them had ever been
healed. I expected this time to be no different.

As a pastor since 1979, I knew you prayed for people who
asked for prayer no matter how impossible the situation might
be. So I prayed. I remember asking her to put her hand over her
eye, and I placed my hand over her hand. I don't even remember exactly what I prayed. It is not important anyway. What is
important is that she had faith and the Holy Spirit fell on her
and healed her.

No words can describe what took place next. As soon as I
removed my hand she started to cry. "I can see your nose; I can
see your face," she screamed.

Incredulously, I exclaimed, "Really?"

"It's not totally clear, but my eye is open!" she cried.

To say the least, I was totally amazed and shocked. I said to
myself, *What is going on here? Could this be the revival I have
been praying for and the one God promised so many years ago?*

It wasn't long before I knew we were in the early stages of
a historical move of God.

39

MAKING IT REAL...PRACTICAL SUGGESTIONS

- Go to the "watering holes" where renewal is taking place. Many conferences feature a renewal emphasis: Toronto, Canada; Brownsville Assembly of God in Pensacola, Florida; The Tabernacle in Melbourne, Florida; The Rock Church in Baltimore, Maryland; Smithton Community Church in Smithton, Missouri; Seattle, Washington; Pasadena, California. I don't fully understand why we have to go, but it seems throughout revival history God visits a place, and by people going there, they receive an impartation from God. Many came to Azusa Street and went back to their home towns and the nations, bringing the Spirit of revival with them.

- Read all you can from the abundance of great literature published as a result of the renewal. Learn about what is happening so you can become both hungrier and more comfortable with it. (See the bibliography in this book for ideas.)

- Invite a speaker who carries the anointing of this renewal to come to your group or church. If you are not a pastor, perhaps you could respectfully suggest to your pastor that a renewal speaker be invited to your church. We have found that some people are contagious "carriers" of this renewal. When they come to a local church, they do impart this renewal to that church.

- "Receive by faith. Take risks. Be persistent. Come as a child. Press in and take what God offers. Soak in the Spirit." These are John Arnott's recommendations for receiving from the current move of God.[6]

- Receive as much as you can and give away as much you can. I have been in renewal since January 1994, and I still cannot satiate the hunger for more of the Holy Spirit. People are constantly praying for me, and

I am also trying to give away this renewal by conducting renewal meetings and conferences around the world. I have learned that the more I give away by praying for people, the more I receive. Share it; it is contagious!

- "The Holy Spirit wants to fill you and enable you to take this renewal everywhere you go."[7]

Notes

1. Azusa Street Revival: The renowned American revival that began in 1906 in Los Angeles and spawned the Pentecostal movement in the United States.
2. *Spread the Fire Anniversary Issue* 4, no. 1 (January 1998). Toronto Airport Christian Fellowship, Toronto, Ontario, Canada.
3. Dr. Guy Chevreau, *Catch the Fire* (London, England: Marshall Pickering, 1994), chap. 4, "The Well Travelled Path."
   Winkie Pratney, *Revival: Its Principles and Personalities* (Lafayette, La.: Huntington House Publishers, 1994), pp. 24-30.
4. John Arnott, *The Father's Blessing* (Lake Mary, Fla.: Creation House, 1995), p. 59.
5. See Chevreau, *Catch the Fire*; Arnott, *The Father's Blessing*; Michael L. Brown, *Let No One Deceive You* (Shippensburg, Pa.: Revival Press, 1997); Wesley Campbell, *Welcoming a Visitation of the Holy Spirit* (Lake Mary, Fla.: Creation House, 1995).
6. Arnott, *The Father's Blessing*, pp. 87-101.
7. Ibid., p. 232.

HARVEST ROCK CHURCH:
A CHURCH BIRTHED

Although Harvest Rock Church (HRC) was officially birthed on April 4, 1994, the vision of starting a new church was initiated by the Lord in November 1993. We were still members of Abundant Life Community Church, where I had resigned as senior pastor and stayed on as staff evangelist.

As we were trying to discover where the Lord would lead us next, my wife and I hoped it would be away from Los Angeles. I had already contacted a real estate agent to appraise our house, but we decided to wait and sell it when we were more sure of the timing of our departure from the church.

While I was away on a speaking engagement in early November, the Lord spoke to me in my spirit that I was not to leave Los Angeles. God began to rebuke me and told me that I was like a Jonah: I was running away from the original call to Los Angeles. I had not fulfilled the task of planting "a church for a great harvest" (see Luke 10:2).

During that same week while I was out of town, the Holy Spirit spoke to my wife and told her also that we were not to leave. A few weeks later, the Lord awakened me at four o'clock in the morning as I heard an inner audible voice ringing in my spirit and my ears, saying, "4-4-94."

My initial interpretation was that would be the date we would be released from our home church. I told this to Sue, and she and I were careful not to share the incident with any-one besides our dear friends Lou and Therese Engle.

Lou, who had been with me at the Vineyard conference, had served with me in the ministry for years and had already left a pastoral position at my same church. He was now heading an organization called Pasadena for Christ, though he and his wife still attended Abundant Life Community Church.

When I shared with Lou and Therese about my Jonah con-viction, they were excited that Sue and I were not leaving Los Angeles, but instead felt directed to begin a new church in the area. We knew that for God to bless us, this new church would have to be true to the initial vision the Lord had spoken to me in the dream so many years ago.

Lou and Therese jumped on board immediately to help us plant the new church. Lou had long held in his heart the dream of revival for Los Angeles, and had decided to continue in the area even if we chose to leave. He was greatly relieved and excited to hear that God was instructing us to return to that same original purpose with him.

AN UNEXPECTED TRANSITION

We decided we would share our decision with the elders of Abundant Life at the end of January. Christmas was coming, and after Christmas I was planning to be away for a month to finish my doctoral dissertation at Fuller Theological Seminary in Pasadena. I thought it would be unwise to open a controversial decision right before the holidays and a month's leave of absence.

Unfortunately, the cat got out of the bag before I had a

chance to share the news properly with all the pastors of the church. To make a long and painful story short, the three other pastors decided it would be best to release us from the church as soon as possible.

The first Sunday of February 1994, we said our good-byes. After 10 long years of plowing in a difficult field, Lou and I, the

■

HARVEST ROCK HAS A YOUTHFUL SOUND THAT
WELL FIT WHAT GOD HAD PUT INTO MY HEART,
BUT I BELIEVE IT HAS A SERIOUS CONNOTATION,
TOO—THAT WE WILL SEE A GREAT HARVEST ON
THIS THRESHOLD GLEANED FOR THE LORD.

45

pastors who had founded the church, along with our wives and families, were officially released.

The momentum of the whole transition left us somewhat shellshocked, and we waited for a month to begin anything new. Both Lou and I had developed an itinerant ministry, so we spoke in other churches during the month of February.

I was now beginning to realize that "4-4-94" did not signify the date we would be released from our former church, but the day we would officially begin our new work in the city.

THE "HARVEST" CONNOTATION

During our interim travels, Lou and I paid a visit to Kansas City, Missouri, to Mike Bickle's church, the Metro Vineyard Fellowship. This is a large, influential church known for its prophetic voice in this hour. We spent some time with Mike and other friends. I was staying at a friend's house nearby, and I asked the Lord one morning during my devotional time about a name for the new church.

I had always liked the word "harvest" and, in fact, had wanted to call our first church "Harvest Community Church." The consensus of the ministry leadership I worked with at the time was that "harvest" was "too agricultural of a name" for a church.

In my heart, I was determined to call this new church "harvest" something or other. I also wanted to reach young people and choose a name to which they could relate. I can't say the Lord spoke to me supernaturally or prophetically, but I clearly heard the name "Harvest Rock Church" resound in my head.

Historically, we know that the harvest was threshed on a rock or large stone and then gleaned. Jesus Himself is called the Rock. Harvest Rock has a youthful sound that well fit what God had put into my heart, but I believe it has a serious connotation, too—that we will see a great harvest on this threshold gleaned for the Lord.

As I shared the name with some of the leaders in Kansas City, everyone I told seemed to like it. Thus, Harvest Rock Church was born!

STARTING AS A PRAYER MEETING

We knew we were officially going to start our new venture in April, but the Lord impressed on me to start a prayer meeting in the month of March in preparation for the new church plant.

One thing we learned in the previous church-planting venture is that a church has to be founded on prayer. Thus, Harvest Rock initially began as a prayer meeting.

Lou and I decided to invite 15 people who were not part of any church to join us. Some of these were former Abundant Life church members who had left for various reasons and were "floating around" and not connected anywhere. Others were simply friends close to us. We were not sure, however, if any of them would attend.

At least the Engles and Ahns would be there, and my own brother, Dr. Chae Woo, a surgeon. To our amazement, exactly 30 people came to our home the first Friday night in March. The next week, more than 65 people came and crammed into our living and dining room. I remember saying to myself, *Where did all these people come from? Who are these people anyway?* I hardly knew any of them!

Yet the word became known because the Holy Spirit was there. We and our families had been moving in renewal, or this

---

THE HOLY SPIRIT FELL ON MANY OF THE PEOPLE ATTENDING. WE COULD SENSE THE POWER AND THE PRESENCE OF THE LORD.... QUITE SIMPLY, THAT IS WHY PEOPLE CAME.

---

fresh outpouring of the Holy Spirit that had become known as the Toronto Blessing, since the end of January, and we were simply inviting the Holy Spirit to attend our prayer meetings.

Our prayer meetings were very simple. We worshiped for a long time, at least an hour. I presented a brief teaching, and then we prayed for the new church. At the end of our prayer time, we prayed for the needs of the people. The Holy Spirit fell on many of the people attending. We could sense the power and the presence of the Lord. They were able to rest in the Holy Spirit and be empowered by His touch. You could see the peace on their faces, and feel the gentle physical, emotional and spiritual refreshing throughout the room. Quite simply, that is why people came.

Though we missed taking a head count for our third prayer meeting in March, the last Friday my wife stopped counting we had 72 people packed like sardines inside our house. We knew we had to find another place to meet.

A pastor in Arcadia, a city next to Pasadena, offered a large building that had plenty of floor space to minister to our people. This was vital because we found out early on that people would fall under the power of the Spirit when we prayed for them. Floor space was not an option! We discovered to our dismay that the building was only available on Saturday nights, but we accepted it anyway.

At the first public meeting, more than 300 people came. We knew most of them were not looking for a new church, but were simply hungry for renewal and came from other churches. God presented Himself powerfully every week. Each Saturday night we prayed, and the Holy Spirit left the floor strewn with people gloriously caught up in the presence of God.

We continued for a few months, but I believed God was requiring me to draw a line and establish a church, not a prayer meeting. So I ministered a word about the church, and asked the people who were coming as members of another church to return to it unless they were sensing God's leading to join Harvest Rock Church.

48 | The following Saturday, only 150 people attended. I was not the least bit discouraged. I knew that these faithful people were interested in becoming a part of Harvest Rock. We did not want a crowd; we wanted to build a church.

The growth of the church was not spectacular, but as we were finishing 1994, 250 people considered HRC their church. Considering my ministry, I thought 1994 turned out to be one of the best years of my life, and really couldn't imagine things getting better. We were experiencing renewal, people were coming to Christ and the church was growing. However, 1994 would be nothing compared to what would take place the following year.

THE TORONTO AIRPORT
VINEYARD CONNECTION

Lou Engle and I finally made it to the Toronto Airport Vineyard Christian Fellowship late in 1994 for its October "Catch the Fire Conference." It was another life-changing experience.

Many things happened at that conference. Perhaps the most significant event was meeting John Arnott, the senior pastor of the Airport Vineyard. Arnott was catapulted into international fame as renewal broke out in his church January 20, 1994.[1] I met him only briefly—informally. I happened to see him unexpectedly in the hall of the hotel where the conference was being held. In that instant of time, I asked him if there was any way he would come to Pasadena during 1995 and conduct renewal meetings. He informed me he had already received more than 300 invitations for the year, and would probably not be able to come. However, he advised me to fax an invitation to him anyway, saying, "You never know."

God knew, though! I went ahead and faxed a letter to him. Just weeks later in December, I received a phone call from his secretary. John would be in San Francisco for the New Year's weekend. He would be willing to come to Pasadena for three days, but it would fall on a Monday through Wednesday. Were we still interested?

Without any hesitation I said yes. Because of the suddenness of the visit, we didn't have time to advertise. Each week, however, I had been meeting with around 25 pastors for prayer, so I presented the idea of cohosting the meetings with John Arnott in January. They all agreed.

We proceeded to rent one of the largest facilities in Pasadena: the Mott Auditorium. The building is named for the respected missionary statesman, John R. Mott, who led the famous Student Volunteer Missions Movement in the United States in the early 1900s—a youth-mobilizing movement that quickly spread to the world and put missions on the map forever. The building is located on the campus of the U.S. Center for World Mission. The campus itself was founded by another missionary statesman, Dr. Ralph Winter.

I will never forget what I saw as I came into the building accompanied by John Arnott that evening of January 2, 1995.

More than 2,000 people had gathered for the meeting. It seemed like a reunion of Christians throughout the Pasadena area. I saw former church members and other people I had not seen for years. It seemed everyone I knew came, plus hundreds more I had never met. The power of God fell. The electric presence of the Holy Spirit permeated the meeting, along with signs, wonders and healings (see 2 Chron. 5:13,14; Acts 2:43). Truly renewal had come not only to our church, but also to the greater Pasadena area.

THE GLENDALE VINEYARD CONNECTION

Again, many significant things happened. For me, the most meaningful was the last meeting John Arnott led on Wednesday of his three-day visit. During the worship time, before John stood up to speak, I distinctly heard God say to me, "You are to be joined with Rick Wright."

Rick was the pastor of the Glendale Vineyard, one of the 25 churches cosponsoring the renewal meetings featuring John Arnott. I really didn't know Rick well, though we had known of each other for years.

Rick was recognized as a prophet in our area, yet we became closer friends only through the renewal. Rick and his wife, Pam, had been to Toronto several times in 1994, and had both been praying for revival for several years. I had met Rick in Toronto in October and had invited him to come to our weekly pastors' prayer meeting. I had also invited him to speak at Harvest Rock Church, and he had asked me to conduct a renewal meeting for his church.

Thus, when God said I was to be joined with Rick, it was somewhat surprising to me and I didn't know exactly what it meant. To my amazement, right after God had spoken to me, Rick walked up to me. He had been sitting a few seats away, and had come with a word for me right in the middle of the worship time. He said, "Ché, the heavens are opened for you, and God is giving you a strategy to reach this city."

I wanted to say, "Rick, you have no idea what you are saying...because this strategy has to do with you!" However, I didn't say a word until later. Lou and I had already planned to spend that Thursday as a day of prayer and fasting, so we invited Rick to join us.

During that time of prayer and fasting, the Lord began to crystallize what He meant by Rick Wright and me being joined together. It would be more than sharing the burden for our city. God was telling us to merge our churches!

We were planning on becoming a Vineyard, so that did not seem to be a problem. The key was who would lead. I had learned in seminary that if churches were going to merge, the only way it would be successful was if one church died to its vision and philosophy of ministry and adopted the other church's philosophy of ministry.

After careful consideration, it seemed best that the Glendale Vineyard would adopt Harvest Rock's vision and mission statement and that I would be the senior pastor. Rick was so hungry for God and His will that he was willing to give up a leadership portion for which he had labored 18 years!

Following much prayer and confirmation from the leaders in the Vineyard, our churches merged and we became Harvest Rock Vineyard in March 1995. That wasn't the only major change to emerge from the meetings with John Arnott, however. John would suggest something else to us that would completely change our lives.

MAKING IT REAL...PRACTICAL SUGGESTIONS

- Bring renewal with you into whatever ministry group you participate.
- If you are a pastor, I would encourage you to create an environment in your services that welcomes the Holy Spirit. I try to do that by using intimate and vertical worship music. (I highly recommend Vineyard worship music, particularly that which was produced between 1994 and 1997.) In my opinion, there seems to also be a strong anointing on worship music by British artists Martin Smith and Matt Redman. Songs produced from Australia under the Hillsongs label, especially those written by Darlene Zschech, are also

very conducive to this current renewal. I also plan a time of personal ministry at the end of every service. We have trained the members of our congregation how to move in renewal prayer and blessing, and we allow them to pray for others at the end of every renewal meeting or at the end of our Sunday morning services.

- As a pastor, you may want to plan a teaching series on related themes such as revival or the Holy Spirit.
- Encourage prophetic ministry in your church, especially in connection with worship. It ushers in the presence of God, as it is the "testimony of Jesus" (Rev. 19:10).
- Be sure to allow time for testimonies in your church service, or other meetings, from people who have been influenced by revival. Nothing tells the story better than firsthand experience.
- Make sure revival is one of your values as a church or ministry. Help your members own that value.

Note
1. John Arnott, *The Father's Blessing* (Lake Mary, Fla.: Creation House, 1995).

THE PROPHETIC CHURCH:
DOING WHAT YOU SEE THE FATHER DO

I believe the key to any successful ministry is to be prophetically led by God Himself. Another way to say this is to "do only what you see the Father doing" (see John 5:19).

Many times we make our plans and ask God to bless them. The better way is to find out what His plans are and align everything else with them. This is why those who abide in Jesus bear much fruit.

As we wait on Him, He reveals His will. When we obey and follow His will, He promises us that we can be assured of bringing forth much fruit (see John 14—15).

This principle is a nonnegotiable of my personal faith and of Harvest Rock Church. Every significant blessing and breakthrough we have enjoyed is a result of obeying this principle, even when things don't make sense. Let me share some examples.

RENEWAL MEETINGS

When John Arnott conducted meetings for us at Mott in January 1995 and saw the number of people who attended, he immediately suggested we begin protracted meetings, just as they had been doing in Toronto since January 1994.

I was not interested in Arnott's suggestion. Our church was less than one year old. In my natural mind, I reasoned that having meetings every night would burn out our people, and eventually kill our young church.

The next month, we invited Wes Campbell to conduct meetings at Mott. He is another powerful brother who shares renewal across the United States. Again, the meetings were tremendously successful, and much fruit was coming forth. Wes also encouraged us to consider protracted meetings.

Sensing that God was saying something to us, and given the imminent merger with Rick Wright and the Vineyard, I opened to the idea of hosting renewal meetings every weekend. I rationalized that after the merger we would have more available leaders and helpers to handle the additional sessions.

The objective was not to usher more people into our building, but to "move with the cloud" of God's presence and provide every opportunity available for Him to bless, refresh and change His people.

As I talked to Rick about the idea of hosting meetings three times a week, he agreed, but also cautioned that more than three might not be healthy for our church. We decided to submit this suggestion to the rest of the pastors with whom we met weekly in prayer, and to share the burden for the renewal. We would discover our conclusion was based on logic and natural thinking—God had other plans. Ironically, He used Rick to change our minds.

I will never forget what happened next. During our prayer meeting, the Holy Spirit began to prophesy through Rick. The Lord gave him the passage in 2 Kings 13, where Elisha encouraged King Jehoahaz to strike the arrow on the ground. The king hit the ground three times. Elisha was furious that the king didn't strike more times. "You should have struck it five or six times," he shouted (see v. 19). As a result, the king won only three battles instead of a complete victory over his enemy.

Rick began to prophesy, "Just as when the King Jehoahaz was told to strike the ground and should have pursued it five or six times, so we are not to have renewal meetings just three times a week—but we are to go five or six nights a week!"

The prophetic word was so powerful, everyone in the room bore witness that God had spoken. It also persuaded me to have faith to start the protracted meetings!

John Arnott had agreed to come back to Pasadena in March, and we agreed that those meetings would launch the nightly renewal meetings. So on March 24, 1995, we began. We met every night for 21 days. From then on, we met five nights a week for more than a year and a half. Today, we have just completed three years of protracted meetings. We are now meeting three nights a week, but we are sensing a new wave coming to our renewal meetings.

Continuing to meet at Mott Auditorium was awkward for me. This had been the facility where the church I had founded and formerly pastored used to meet. Although they had moved from that particular building, they were located just across the campus from us on the U.S. Center for World Mission.

Because the protracted meetings involved several other churches, and because Harvest Rock Church met in another city, it made the most sense to meet at the auditorium. I would have never dreamed the Lord would ask us to move our church into Mott, but that is exactly what happened next.

MOVING TO MOTT

"Ché, I know you don't sense this, but I really believe that God wants us to move our church into Mott." I must have heard that at least a half a dozen times from my friend and fellow pastor, Lou Engle. It wasn't because Lou lived across the street from Mott, which he did. Lou felt prophetically that Mott had been dedicated by the Nazarenes for revival, and God was going to visit it again.

He sensed it was crucial for our church to be based at Mott in order to usher in and experience the fullness of the historic move of God we had been believing would happen. Frankly, I wanted nothing to do with moving Harvest Rock—especially to a location just across the lawn from my former church. Emphatically, and almost angrily, I resisted the idea.

In addition, it made no sense to me to rent Mott for our church services. True, the renewal meetings were able to handle their share of the large building's rent, but having to pay more rent for the auditorium was a totally different proposition.

After all, the Glendale Vineyard with whom we were merging was bringing with it a significant mortgage on the building it owned. Because we could meet there, what sense did it make to rent Mott on Sundays?

God again would ask me to do that which boggles the rational mind. Jim Goll, a good friend and respected prophetic minister from Kansas City, Missouri, called me.

"Ché, I had a dream about you last night. I saw you holding a bottle of Mott's Applesauce...does this mean anything to you?" he mused.

"You wouldn't believe it if I told you," I replied. "Lou and I have been considering whether or not the Lord is leading us to move our church into a building called Mott Auditorium. As far as I am concerned, there is no way that we can afford it. Besides, it is too close to my former church. I just don't think it would be right to move there," I added with firm conviction. I thought I had done a pretty good job of at least convincing myself.

"Now I know what the dream means," Jim countered. "Ché, you are holding 'Mott' in your hands. I believe God wants you to possess Mott Auditorium. The applesauce means you will bear fruit as you do. Furthermore, I am sensing that the Lord will provide for you, so you don't have to worry about your expenses—and He will also take care of your situation with your former church."

I must say that obeying God in moving into Mott Auditorium was one of the most difficult and humiliating decisions I have made since planting Harvest Rock Church. It was especially difficult because I had told the new pastor of my former church that I was not interested in moving into Mott.

■

JUST AS HOLDING PROTRACTED MEETINGS MADE
NO SENSE INITIALLY, BUT BORE TREMENDOUS
FRUIT, SO I REALIZE IN LOOKING BACK AT THE
LAST FEW YEARS THAT MOVING TO MOTT WAS
ALSO THE RIGHT DECISION.

When God spoke, I knew I had to humble myself before that pastor and ask to be released from that word. I asked the Lord if this was a situation in which I should instead "swear to my own hurt" (see Ps. 15:4) and not consider any move to Mott, but through the prophetic words and godly counsel, He directed me otherwise.

I had already made a commitment when we started the work that we would "only do what we saw the Father do" (see John 5:19), so I had to go forward with what it seemed He was saying now.

Just as holding protracted meetings made no sense initially, but bore tremendous fruit, so I realize in looking back at the last few years that moving to Mott was also the right decision.

God would confirm His leading again a month after Jim Goll had called.

AN ANGELIC VISITATION

On May 28, 1995, Mott experienced an extraordinary visitation.

My daughter Joy, who was 12 at that time, and her best friend Christine had just returned from the renewal meetings and were full of the Holy Spirit. It was late when they came home, and I was just about asleep when I heard laughter and banging in the family room next to our bedroom.

The girls were "camping out" on their sleeping bags in the family room, but were manifesting and shaking so much under the power of the Holy Spirit that they were banging loudly on the floor.

Although this was wonderful and I was happy for them, they were making so much noise that I couldn't sleep. I had to get up early the next day and preach the Sunday message so I needed a good night's rest.

I went into the family room and politely asked them to be quiet. They apologized and said they would. I went back to bed.

Fifteen minutes later, I heard them banging and laughing again. I have to be honest; by this time I was upset. I marched into the room and said sternly, "I'm glad you are having a wonderful time. But if you're going to manifest, go to your bedroom and manifest all you want, but don't do it right next to my bedroom!" Once again they apologized, so I went back to sleep and didn't hear another peep.

I discovered the next morning that things became quiet because something far more wonderful happened. My wife, who had been helping me quiet the girls, realized the Holy Spirit was doing something unique with them.

She listened while Christine began to prophesy, "Mott, Mott, we've got to go to Mott!"

It was almost one o'clock in the morning. Not wanting to disturb me any further, and knowing the Lord was moving on these children, Sue drove the girls to the auditorium.

The moment she unlocked the door to the building, she sensed the glory of God, and saw a white mist and angels throughout the auditorium. The girls' eyes widened in awe. As they looked up, they began to describe seeing thousands of doves everywhere, and hundreds of angels of every size and ethnic color!

Sue quickly went across the street and rapped on the Engles's door. Lou came over to Mott, and he, too, could sense the strong presence of the Holy Spirit, but saw nothing. Only the two little girls and Sue could see the angels and doves, along with flowers and other wonders. It was like a scene from the book of Acts, where angelic visitations were common.

Lou decided to separate the girls and test them to see if they were seeing the same thing. He would ask, "What are you seeing in that corner?"

Each would say "an angel." Then she would describe the very same angel without any collaboration from her friend. Sue also confirmed what they were seeing. Each saw and described flowers like no flowers that exist on earth. The flowers appeared as jewelry, but in vibrant colors they had never seen before.

Christine and Joy saw thousands of doves. Several sat on each seat in the vast auditorium, and many more hanging like bats on the ceiling of a cave. They saw many other incredible things, but the most impressive to them were the angels.

They described the angels as warring angels. They saw giant angels, and infant angels as cherubs. This visitation lasted for almost six months. Other children also saw the angels at Mott.

I asked my daughter to lay her hands on me, but I was still unable to see anything. The promise from God is that He will "pour out His Spirit on our sons and our daughters, and they would prophesy. Young people would see visions" (see Joel 2:28). This is exactly what happened. Our youth, however, would not be the only ones guided by the Spirit's lead.

OUR STAFF GROWS

God continued to lead us in a prophetic manner—supernaturally revealing exact details we needed to know about how to continue this work right when we needed to know them.

As Graham Cooke states in his book *Developing Your Prophetic Gifting,* "Prophetic ministry is concerned with the church, and it is concerned with the direction we take, as well as who will lead and how we will get to our destination. Prophetic ministry brings God's perspective, releases vision and calling and undermines your enemy. It is concerned with the church fulfilling its call."[1] The Lord did not disappoint us.

When we began the protracted meetings, we desperately needed to hire a full-time administrator to cover the renewal meetings and the church. I had no clue how to begin looking for the right person who had both the appropriate spiritual and natural skills.

After we had decided to hire an administrator, my wife received an open vision from heaven. It was a clear visual picture,

■

IF WE WILL FOLLOW THE LORD'S PROMPTING,

EACH OF US HAS AN EQUAL OPPORTUNITY

CONTINUALLY TO STEP INTO THE BEST "FIT"

FOR HIS PURPOSES AND OUR NEEDS.

almost like a daydream, that appeared real and was how God chose to speak to Sue that day about a decision we needed to make (see Acts 10:11). She saw Jeff Wright, the brother of Rick Wright, walking around Mott auditorium holding a clipboard in his hand. She knew immediately that Jeff was to be our administrator.

When Sue told me the vision, I knew it was of God. Just a few months earlier, Rick's wife, Pam, had submitted a prophetic word to me that Sue had never heard. Pam said she sensed that one day Jeff was to join our staff. So I called Jeff and asked if he could meet with me right away.

When I shared Sue's vision with Jeff, as well as Pam's prophetic word, he broke down and began to cry. Jeff knew he was called, but had no idea how that would be fulfilled in his life. Twelve years prior, he had received a word from the internationally known prophet, Dr. Bill Hamon, that he would serve the Lord in vocational ministry. Because no door appeared to open, he had been faithful to serve wholeheartedly and had much success in the business world—and all the while God reminded him of his call.

Now this word was coming to pass. Jeff has not only become one of my closest friends, but he has also been the best administrative pastor I have ever known on any staff. It simply proves that if we will follow the Lord's prompting, each of us has an equal opportunity continually to step into the best "fit" for His purposes and our needs.

This truth soon happened again—on a bigger scale. Just after our merger with the Glendale Vineyard, we invited Jim Goll to come to Pasadena again and minister at the renewal meetings. In a special session with our leaders, Jim began a time of prophetic ministry. He prophesied that more churches would merge with Harvest Rock.

Lou and I knew immediately which two of those churches were. We had developed a strong relationship with Jim and Laura Johnston, the pastors of Cornerstone Christian Fellowship, and Karl and Debbie Malouff, the pastors of Community Bible Church. Both churches had been influenced powerfully by the renewal. Together, they had been helping to cosponsor the ongoing meetings with us, as were several other churches in our area.

Something was different about the Johnstons and the Malouffs, however. They were more involved than others, and our connection with them was more extensive. Each had committed their worship teams and church members to help staff the renewal meetings. Jim had already begun speaking at the evening meetings to help in the rotation with Lou, Rick and me.

What is more, God had already spoken to both Jim and Karl about merging with us before Jim Goll gave the prophetic word. We just had not had an opportunity to talk about it together yet. We all merged in September 1995—adding two more excellent pastoral couples to our staff.

As of this writing, a Hispanic church, pastored by my good friends Carlos and Brenda Quintero, has also sensed a call to merge with Harvest Rock Church. To confirm this desire, the Quinteros' denominational leaders have blessed and released the entire congregation to join our church. Although their fellowship will still structurally function much as before, it will now fall under the Harvest Rock covering.

Looking back, I am amazed at the sovereign work of God to bring about such a merger, and at the love and unity we have experienced together as pastors. It has been an awesome and humbling thing, and one I know does not happen often. Pastors Rick, Jim, Karl and Carlos truly are to be commended for their humility and their willingness to lay down their positions as senior pastors to serve another senior pastor.

Although I know it was not altogether easy for everyone, I have no doubt that God brought us together and supernaturally has knit a team of complementary men and ministries, which continues to influence our local fellowship and other churches around the world.

LEAVING THE VINEYARD

Just after our merger with the Glendale Vineyard in March, we changed our name from Harvest Rock Church to Harvest Rock Vineyard.

In April, I received another phone call from Jim Goll. He had another prophetic insight to share. Jim consistently had significant and instructive words that proved foundational to us at Harvest Rock, but we would have to wait nine months to understand this one.

"Ché, I had an open vision pertaining to you as I was in my living room. I heard a cork popping, and saw you with a rose wine bottle. On the front of the bottle was written "nine months." The bottle had been shaken, and the cork popped out. The wine had changed in the bottle. You were now holding another substance."

I dearly love the prophetic, but I didn't have a clue what Jim was talking about. What frustrated me more was that Jim had been given an interpretation of the word, but the Lord would not release him to share it with me. He said he would call in nine months to tell me the rest of the story.

In the interim, I forgot about the dream. The next nine months presented myriad blessings and challenges that were consuming in their own right. The renewal meetings were gaining momentum, but so was the criticism of people who did not like what was happening in Toronto and at Mott.[2]

Many were calling this a counterfeit revival. In my opinion, the persecution and the distractions adversely affected the national leaders of the Vineyard, which resulted in their request for the Toronto church to withdraw from its association with Vineyard.

Like many others, I was shocked at the request made of the Toronto church in October 1995. On December 8, Lou, Rick and I met with the leaders of the Vineyard. We thought we would also be asked to drop our association with the movement.

As we were driving to Anaheim, we were discussing our options. I had just finished saying we needed to continue the renewal meetings, regardless of the outcome of our appointment.

It was too obvious that God had initiated the work and that we must continue in it—even if it meant leaving the Vineyard. I concluded by saying, "At least we know that God has brought us together for this work."

No sooner had the words passed from my lips when a black Mercedes passed us bearing a license plate that read: RICK CHE. Talk about a confirmation that our merger was God's doing!

I screamed, "Look at the license plate on that car!" Both Rick and Lou also started to scream and manifest as the Holy Spirit hit us. Although it may seem like a small incident to someone else, it served as a sign to us and gave us tremendous faith as we met with the leadership of the Vineyard.

God seemed to be saying, "I initiated the renewal meetings. I brought the churches together. I am the head of Harvest Rock, and I am with you." As it turned out, the leaders of the Vineyard did not ask us to leave. To quote a Vineyard leader, perhaps "a happy parting of the ways" might indeed be the best solution for everyone. We agreed. Thus, on December 8, following the day of infamy for Pearl Harbor and the world, Harvest Rock ceased to be a Vineyard.

A week later, Jim Goll called. "Ché, do you remember the vision I had about you and a rose wine bottle upon which was written 'nine months' and the bottle's cork popping open?" he pressed.

"Yes," I haltingly replied, vaguely remembering the conversation those many months before.

"Here is the interpretation of the vision. But before I share it with you, I want to ask you how long you were with the Vineyard," Jim continued.

I remember having to count out the months on my fingers as I held the phone. "Nine months," I finally replied.

"Well, don't you get it?" Jim queried. I still didn't know what he was talking about.

Jim was happy to clue me in. "Well...the wine bottle represents your church. You were a 'Vineyard,' and after nine months the cork popped open, and I saw that the wine had changed and became a new substance. You were no longer a 'Vineyard.' Get it?

"God told me through the vision that you would be part of the Vineyard for only nine months. I wanted to tell you the interpretation, but He wouldn't let me. It could have been interpreted as being divisive if I told you before that you would be leaving a movement within such a short time. That is why I could only share the vision, and then wait nine months to give you the interpretation," he concluded.

I was absolutely stunned by this. Several things went through my mind. My first thought was that Jim is an incredibly prophetic brother who receives accurate specifics from the Lord. I was very grateful for the tremendous comfort and encouragement his words had given me. Indeed, God had sovereignly called us to become a Vineyard, and then had sovereignly led us out.

There is no substitute for the peace you have in knowing God is with you in the difficult transitions that often accompany ministry. How anyone can lead without the grace and support found through solid prophetic revelation and confirmation is a mystery to me. Thank God He chooses to use this vehicle of ministry. As Dr. Bill Hamon says, "The prophetic ministry is one of the nearest and dearest ministries to the heart of God."[3]

To this day, I am thankful God did lead us to be a Vineyard Church, though for such a short time. I love the Vineyard movement and its leadership. I have a deep love and respect for Bob Fulton, Todd Hunter and many other leaders of the Vineyard, and most especially for the late John Wimber. His love for the Church, his revelation of worship and his fruit as a gifted renewal leader have left a rich legacy for the Body of Christ. I, for one, am most grateful. I have no doubt that our unique "spiritual DNA" was developed in part through many wonderful values we received from our association with the Vineyard movement.

I am also grateful that God led us on from the Vineyard, because He had other plans, and another movement. It would be a movement He would allow me the privilege of starting and leading—and one that would encompass what He had placed in my heart many long years ago. It would be a vision for the nations.

MAKING IT REAL...PRACTICAL SUGGESTIONS

- Welcome this prophetic move of God and do all you can to receive prophetic ministers and learn about what God is doing in this hour.
- Attend a conference on the prophetic, and/or enroll in a course that teaches how to move in the prophetic. (A course about the prophetic will be taught at our Harvest International School of Ministry.)
- Be mentored by a prophetic person.
- Raise up faithful prophetic intercessors.
- Read books such as *The Elijah Task* by John and Paula Sandford; *Prophets and Personal Prophecy* by Dr. Bill Hamon; *Developing Your Prophetic Gifting* by Graham

Cooke; *User Friendly Prophecy* by Larry Randolph;
The Voice of God by Cindy Jacobs.

- Be careful not to direct the move of God in your church or ministry on your own terms or expectations. Make it your aim to flow with "what you see the Father doing."
- Allow God to bring the personal "flavor" of renewal He intends for you and your church rather than looking to imitate what you have seen elsewhere.

Notes

1. Graham Cooke, *Developing Your Prophetic Gifting* (Kent, England: Sovereign World International, 1994), p. 194.
2. Michael L. Brown, *Let No One Deceive You* (Shippensburg, Pa.: Revival Press, 1997).
3. Bill Hamon, *Prophets and Personal Prophecy* (Shippensburg, Pa. Destiny Image Publishers, 1987), p. 17.

CHAPTER FOUR

HARVEST INTERNATIONAL MINISTRIES: A VISION FOR THE WORLD

Harvest Rock Church had joined the Vineyard for life. We had no intention of joining or starting another movement. Why reinvent the wheel? The Vineyard loved the renewal and was planting churches around the world.

The leadership had shared with me a desire to plant 500 churches in Asia alone. I was sold; so we became a Vineyard. Who would have guessed that we would be out of the Vineyard after only nine months?

Life is not perfect, nor is it predictable. People change, and so do movements. When the leaders had asked John Arnott and the Toronto church to leave the movement, we thought it was best for us to leave, too.

Now the big question became: Where do we belong? I had

always believed in accountability and spiritual covering. The natural decision was to go with John Arnott.

John was planning to start his own movement, which he eventually did, called Partners in Harvest. A small number of Vineyard churches left when the Toronto church was ousted, and they immediately looked to John and Carol Arnott for leadership.

Many independent churches affected by the renewal also joined Partners in Harvest as soon as they heard about it. In addition, John had personally invited me to be part of the new movement. It made total sense to join him and his movement.

After all, we had both been Vineyard churches that loved the renewal. In effect, John had also been the spiritual father of our own renewal meetings. He had been the first to help us organize the citywide gatherings in Pasadena. In addition, we deeply loved and respected John and Carol, and had become good friends within a short time.

John was planning an inaugural meeting with the pastors who were interested in Partners. It was to coincide with the third anniversary celebrating the birth of the Toronto renewal. I bought my airline ticket prepared to fly to Canada in January, join the celebration and officially join Partners in Harvest. Again, I received a phone call that would change all my plans.

A Prophetic Word About a New Movement

Up till this point, I had received only one phone call from Cindy Jacobs. She had shared the amazing and accurate prophetic word regarding my departure from the ministry organization I had served for many years. Now it was the end of December 1995, and she was calling again.

Cindy had heard that we were no longer a Vineyard. Once again, she delivered a strong prophetic directive that would change the destiny of our ministry.

"Ché, you are not to join another movement. The Lord has called you to be a father of your own movement. He has called you to be an Abraham, and out of your loins, you will be a father to many," she declared.

Her words exploded in my heart. Years earlier, when she had come to speak at Abundant Life Church while I was the pastor, she had given me the same word. In fact, I had kept a written copy of it. I had often pondered her word in my heart, just as Mary of old (see Luke 2:19). Yet because of my own insecurities, I did not see how it could ever come to fruition.

Now I was hearing it again. Things had changed, and my plans to be a Vineyard for life had fallen through. I knew that God had something else in store for me—but starting my own movement was the farthest thing from my mind. Though I still had my doubts, something inside told me this was the word of the Lord.

When I shared the word with my wife and the pastoral staff, each bore witness to its accuracy. My fellow pastor Rick Wright, himself a prophet, said that we should not only obey the word, but should also share it with John Arnott.

So in late January, Rick and I flew to Toronto for the scheduled kickoff of Partners in Harvest. In addition to this celebration, a meeting was scheduled with other leaders from around the world who were interested in networking the renewal to other parts of the globe and wished to provide international leadership for it.

It was an honor to be in these gatherings, but I was very apprehensive about meeting with John Arnott. I was not looking forward to sharing the news that we were not planning to become part of Partners in Harvest.

I was hesitant because similar encounters with other people in my past had ended in rejection. Had I known how graciously John would respond, I never would have given it a second thought.

When we did speak, I shared Cindy's word and what I believed God was speaking to me. John and Carol responded in a most godly release. We all shared disappointment that we would not be working intimately together, but both of them encouraged me to follow God's prophetic leading.

To this day we remain close to the Arnotts. They have not only opened their pulpit to us in Toronto, but they have also asked me to share the same platform with them in Indonesia and in South Korea. They are some of the most loving people I have ever met. No wonder God continues to use them powerfully around the world.

HARVEST INTERNATIONAL MINISTRIES

We needed a name for our movement. Again, I don't know if God inspired the name or if it was breathed from my spirit, but "Harvest International Ministries" came to me loud and clear.

■

70 | WE WERE BELIEVING GOD FOR A GREAT

INTERNATIONAL HARVEST....THIS MINISTRY

WAS ALSO TO BE ALL ABOUT *HIM*—JESUS.

It seemed to be a perfect name. First, we were believing God for a great international harvest. Second, the first letters of each word spell "H-I-M." This ministry was also to be all about *Him*—Jesus.

We did a legal search for the name, and to my surprise, no one was using the name in California. So we incorporated as a nonprofit mission agency.

H.I.M. was born, and the vision I had always held to go to the nations sharing the gospel was now becoming a reality. God was placing in my heart ideas for how it would happen.

The model impressive to me as a New Testament church is found at Antioch. The Antioch church sent Paul and Barnabas as the first apostolic team to plant churches in unreached areas of the known world at that time (see Acts 13).

The Antioch church consisted of a plurality of multiethnic and prophetic leaders committed to worship, prayer and missions. We had begun Harvest Rock Church on this same premise. We taught that the church existed for missions, and our vision was to send church planters throughout the world.

We also believed it was providential for Harvest Rock to be located on the campus of the U.S. Center for World Mission. The Center's founders, missionaries Ralph and Roberta Winter, have brought major clarity and fruit to the Body of Christ and the Great Commission by targeting the remaining unreached people groups as their focus.

This clearly defined our priority for H.I.M. The first missionaries officially sent out by Harvest Rock Church and H.I.M. were Jamie and Chiho Harris—they were sent to a 2.5 million unreached people group in Asia. For security and safety reasons, I am not at liberty to say anything more about the work.

As much as unreached peoples are a priority, however, we must respond to the fullness of what the Father bids us do. Thus, we include frequently reached nations, and plant churches as the Holy Spirit directs.

One thing God has made clear to us is to invite other churches to be partners with us in fulfilling the task. We realized that as a local church we could only do so much. If we network with hundreds of other like-minded churches, however, we will have enough resources to cause serious damage to Satan's kingdom by planting churches around the world. We want to be a part of what God is doing today and how God is doing it.

Dr. Peter Wagner, an author and internationally respected leader in church growth, views it this way: "Church growth analysts are beginning to identify apostolic networks as a modern movement. World-changing leaders and movements are arising to establish progressive structures for families of churches and ministries."[1] That is why our October "Catch the Fire" conference at Mott Auditorium in 1996 became a watershed week for H.I.M.

We invited several independent churches to meet with us a day before the conference officially started. We shared the vision of H.I.M. and invited any interested churches to link with us. To my surprise, many did.

What God has done is truly amazing. At this writing, more than 140 churches are official members of H.I.M., and many more are closely affiliated as "friends" of H.I.M. It is one of the many "apostolic networks" God is raising up to be the wineskin for the great harvest. I know this is only the beginning of another tremendous move of God to expand the kingdom through church planting around the globe!

NETWORKING THE APOSTLES TOGETHER

For a major revival to occur, or for the Body of Christ world-wide to move into the leadership of overseeing millions won to Christ, those whom God has set as foundational in building His Church must arise (see Eph. 3:20). This is a critical hour for the apostles to take their places.

■

ONE REASON H.I.M. HAS GROWN SO QUICKLY IS THAT GOD HAS BROUGHT TOGETHER MANY "BUDDING" APOSTLES UNDER ITS UMBRELLA.

Dr. Wagner, commenting in David Cannistraci's book *Apostles and the Emerging Apostolic Movement*, believes "we can begin to approach the spiritual vitality and power of the first-century church *only* if we recognize, accept, receive and minister in all the spiritual gifts, including the gift of apostle."[2] Wagner believes one way to recognize a modern-day apostle is to find a person who is looked to by many churches for leadership. Usually these churches are ones the person has helped plant either directly or indirectly.

One reason H.I.M. has grown so quickly is that God has brought together many "budding" apostles under its umbrella. I say "budding" because these leaders are still in development and still coming into the fullness of their ministries, much like me.

The first apostle to join us was David Gama of Malawi. Rick Wright had developed a significant ministry in Africa for years, and one of his vital covenant relationships was with this man. When our churches merged, David was a part of the merger.

I was glad to have David join the team. Years ago, God had revealed to me that I would be involved with Africa. I just didn't know how or when. What I didn't know is that David Gama had planted many churches—all of which he wanted to bring into H.I.M.

We gave him additional funds to plant more churches. In the short time since David has joined us, he has sown more than 20 additional congregations—the smallest numbering 45 adults! Thus, H.I.M. encompasses nearly 80 vibrant churches in Africa alone.

73

The next budding apostle to join us was Jan Palmer of Vienna, Austria. Jan, who was born in Jamaica, is an amazing young man. While studying in Europe, he established a Bible study that eventually became a church. He has since planted seven churches in Europe. One is pastored by good friends of mine, Eric and Crissy Tamaru. They were a part of church-planting efforts by the former organization I had served, and had become stranded when the missions vision was curtailed overseas. When they heard I was involved in starting a new missions movement, Eric came with Jan to our first "Catch the Fire" conference. They both joined H.I.M. and added their churches to the roster.

Another recent apostle to join H.I.M. is Terry Edwards. Terry pastors Lake Tahoe Christian Fellowship, the largest charismatic church in South Lake Tahoe, California. He is also the president of Christian Equippers International (CEI), and an author of many of its materials. CEI has produced many excellent seminars and materials about evangelism and discipleship, including the "Glad Tidings School of Evangelism Seminar," which I consider among the best.

Terry is also a remarkable church planter who has fathered many churches in the United States and in the Philippines. When Terry joined H.I.M., we gained 20 churches in the Philippines.

To help us reach five continents, the Lord has most recently added Dennis Walker—a wonderful man who administers 14 churches in Peru, which have now become a part of our network.

Paul and Catherine Lee, the Korean pastors at Harvest Rock Church, were sent to South Korea on March 23, 1998 to oversee the five H.I.M. churches there. They also took food and medical supplies into North Korea in preparation for planting churches there when the doors open.

74

That means we now have established churches on the continents of Asia, Africa, Europe, South America and North America. When I look at the quality of leaders God has added to H.I.M., I am truly amazed. Although we are privileged to be joined with such wonderful churches and those yet desiring to be part of H.I.M., our ultimate goal reaches much further. Through the power of the Holy Spirit, we desire to train and send multitudes more missionaries and church planters to the ends of the earth.

HARVEST INTERNATIONAL SCHOOL

As of this writing, serious plans are under way to establish a one-year training school to prepare church planters for ministry. Although I am grateful to have personally completed both a master's and a doctoral program at Fuller Theological Seminary, I do believe there are easier and less costly alternatives to prepare more people for ministry.

Too often I have witnessed young men and women called to the mission field miss their objectives. After four years of seminary training, they feel obligated to work and pay off their student loans before endeavoring any missions venture. In the interim they begin families, and often find it too difficult to go to the mission field.

I believe people can and should be groomed for ministry in the setting of their local church. As people grow in character and maturity, they should be given various levels of leadership responsibilities in the church as part of their training. I do believe, however, in a need for specialized training for anyone desiring to minister overseas or in a cross-cultural setting. That will be the intent of our school.

For those people recommended by their pastors to attend, our school will equip them with tools to apply the Word of God accurately, communicate the Scriptures, cast out demons, pray for physical and inner healing, and plant a growing church cross-culturally.

The school will be immensely practical and inexpensive. If you would like a free catalogue for the school, please contact us at:

75

Harvest International School
1539 E. Howard Street
Pasadena, CA 91104

MAKING IT REAL...PRACTICAL SUGGESTIONS

- Learn about what God is doing throughout the Body of Christ internationally to bring the various streams together. Read books about other streams and movements; listen to tapes and watch videos or attend church services in other places. Embrace this hour of "cross-pollination" as God causes His diverse Body to become one in His love and glory.
- Read books to help you understand the apostolic ministry, such as *Apostles and the Emerging Apostolic Movement* by David Cannistraci.
- Determine what relationships God is putting before you and what links the Holy Spirit is creating for you.

Invest yourself in learning what plans God may have for you in this regard.

- Network with other apostolic networks. Join one if yours is an independent church, or you are in a position to do so. If appropriate, pray about starting your own network.
- Consider becoming an affiliate "Friend of H.I.M." (Harvest International Ministries).

Notes

1. David Cannistraci, *Apostles and the Emerging Apostolic Movement* (Ventura, Calif.: Regal Books, 1996), p. 188.
2. Ibid., p. 12.

REMARKABLE HEALINGS

"Pastor, we think our friend is demon possessed (see Luke 8:27)! Could you please come and minister to her?"

My heart sank. It was only our second citywide renewal meeting in Pasadena. More than 1,000 people had come that particular night. People were being ministered to wonderfully and joyfully on the gymnasium floor of Mott Auditorium, and the last thing I wanted to do was to shift gears and pray for someone's deliverance. Yet I quickly followed the small band of Korean students who had come to me for help.

A KOREAN STUDENT'S MIRACLE

They led me to another young Korean student, around 20 years old, who was lying on the floor. She was definitely manifesting, but I could discern the manifestation was not demonic but rather a powerful touch of the Holy Spirit. She was shaking and speaking in tongues.

I immediately reassured her friends that this was not the work of the devil, but the sovereign hand of God, and encouraged them to remain with her and pray for her as she continued to receive from the Lord.

Because this visitation was so new to everyone, many people thought early on that some of the manifestations looked demonic. We soon learned from the fruit of changed lives and marvelous healings that these unusual displays were from the Holy Spirit (see Matt. 12:33). This proved to be true in this situation as well.

I did not know what had happened to this young Korean girl until a few weeks later when her pastor, Robert Oh, told me. He had come to Mott with his whole congregation and helped pray for and witness what happened to his young congregant that night.

He explained that this student had severe scoliosis and was, in fact, encouraged to have surgery. While she was on the floor at Mott, God gave her a new prayer language and healed her back! The following week when the doctors took X rays, they were dumbfounded. They could not believe that her back was straight. She asked the doctors for the X rays, and she brought them to her pastor to show him the results of prayer that night at Mott. The pastor was so impressed that he not only shared this story with me, but he also felt led by the Lord to give us a check for $4,000 to support the renewal meetings we were conducting!

This is only one of many incredible miracles that have occurred at Mott.

A MIRACLE HEALING OF MULTIPLE SCLEROSIS

Another is the story of Brenda Quintero, who shared these words firsthand in the September 1995 issue of our newsletter, *Harvest Times*:

> A few years ago, I felt like I was given a death sentence. I was diagnosed with multiple sclerosis (MS). It is a neurological disease that affects the central nervous system. The body begins to destroy itself, one nerve and muscle at a time.

There was really nothing that the doctors could do to stop the progress of this horrible torment, except advise me to avoid stressful situations. While that seemed impossible to anyone living in this day and age, I tried to more effectively manage my stress. As a real estate agent, I needed to show property to clients, but eventually I could not even do that because my right foot would drag. Soon, even walking up and down the steps at my office became difficult, so my desk had to be moved to the ground floor.

All the while, Satan repeatedly whispered things like, "You rebelled against God. You put other things first. After He died for you, you counted His death for nothing. You can't be healed. You don't deserve His kindness." The words weren't always the same, but the message was clear. I was a born again Christian and believed with all my heart that God could heal me. But eventually I gave in and agreed with the accuser's lies thinking that I was not worthy of God's mercy and healing hand.

After a couple of years of living under these lies, I realized that I did not have to be perfect to receive from God. God began a transformation in me as He showed me tangibly His love and His wonderful presence night after night through the renewal meetings and the Word coming forth every day.

I prayed anew that He would take complete control of my life and admitted I had been rebellious. The Lord began a deep cleansing in me, and gave me a double portion of His Holy Spirit. As I yielded and obeyed God more, His presence in my life increased and became more and more real as the months passed. It is like I became a "reborn" born-again believer!

Yet even though things were changing on the inside, nothing had changed for the better in my body. In fact, things seemed to get worse. May 9th was a particularly bad day for me physically. I had to lean on my husband to make it into the renewal services at Mott Auditorium. As I was listening to the message, my right leg began to spasm uncontrollably.

I cried out before the Lord to remove this abomination from me. Later a dear friend of mine told me as I cried that the Lord would heal me when it would give Him the most glory. I suddenly began to think of all the stages of MS: a walker, a wheelchair, then being bedridden. I reasoned that the most dramatic healing would be after I became bedridden, so I prepared myself for this probability.

Two days later at Mott, a woman who was blind in one eye and had only partial sight in the other eye was healed. When I saw the power of the Lord at work and felt the incredible anointing of the Holy Spirit, I asked my husband to pray for me right that second. I fell to the floor under the power of the Spirit and lay resting there for a few minutes as were others around me.

Soon I got up and went to take my place as part of the prayer team to minister to others who had come to receive at the meeting. I didn't notice anything different than I had felt at any previous times of prayer.

About 11 p.m., I had finished praying for others when the Lord spoke loudly into my spirit and said, "Take off your shoes and run." I reasoned with God saying that if He hadn't healed me, I would fall flat on my face. Again I heard..."Take off your shoes and run."

I decided to go for it! I took off my shoes and went full speed ahead! It was absolutely incredible! I didn't fall! In fact, I ran around the auditorium twice before I came to my husband and said breathlessly, "Honey, I think I'm healed!" My husband asked me to run again— so I did! Then we began telling everyone what had just happened! It was a miracle—God had healed me!

I really can't describe the change. Two days earlier, I had taken a hard fall while just walking through my house. Now I was running! I was doing things I hadn't done in years—I skipped, I jumped, I ran, and I danced before the Lord—laughing all the while because the enemy was defeated!

I'll never be the same—body, soul or spirit! God's mercy triumphed—and He healed me! Praise the Lord!

Others had to hold on in faith, too, for their healings, but their miracles also came at Mott.

A REMARKABLE HEALING "IN ITS TIME"

One of our church members also shared her saga in the February 1996 issue of our newsletter, *Harvest Times*:

Angeles Peart had suffered with a back problems for years. Two herniated disks had often rendered her unable to work, and generated such severe pain that she often could not move. Prescription drugs helped temporarily ease the knife-like throbbing, but soon the ravaging cycle began again and brought with it even more discouragement.

Yet Angeles continued to pursue the Lord for healing, struggling all the way and wondering what the failure was on her part. By the time we held a healing conference in October, 1995, Angeles had all but given up hope. Two years of devastating pain had been a long time.

She had been to a chiropractor and submitted to the treatments; no success. Then to an orthopedic surgeon, with no success. Next, a neurosurgeon, MRI testing, and more treatments. Still no success. What's more, the doctor stated he did not want to perform the surgery necessary to relieve the pain. Angeles saw her doors of hope shutting quickly.

In desperation, she tried one more chiropractor recommended by a friend. During his initial evaluation, this doctor remarked that Angeles should not even be able to walk. Her herniated disks at L4 and L5 on the spine were deteriorated to the point of bone on bone.

Angeles came to the healing conference doing her best to try and believe God would still come through somehow. Tim Storey, a well-known healing evangelist, ministered the first night. In his unusual style, he asked people to race to the altar and receive from the Lord. Later, as people testified, Angeles heard that God was moving and many were being healed.

She thought perhaps Friday would be her day. Again, Storey asked people at the next service to rush to the front to receive their healing. He called forward those who were in severe need of pain and everyone seemed to point to Angeles. She marched hurriedly forward full of anticipation when Tim Storey gazed at her and said, "It's not your time yet."

Angeles tried to keep her composure. She kept thinking to herself, "Any moment now..." She was still hoping as she returned to her seat believing perhaps she'd be "the finale."

Yet she was left waiting as the service ended. She went to the car, collapsing in a sea of tears and rejection. Her husband raced to find Tim Storey. The Lord jogged Tim's mind, and he made a bee line for the car to the woman he had forgotten. He grabbed Angeles' hands and said, "Look at me!" She could hardly lift up her head. "Look at me!"

She made an effort and Tim began to pray. Her faith had hit rock bottom. According to her husband, Ray, you could have "offered her a million dollars and it wouldn't have made a difference."

As quickly as the prayer had begun, it was over, and Tim left. Angeles tried to clear her mind of the sorrow she felt and assess the situation. Nothing happened...yet.

As the conference continued, Randy Clark, the pastor

God used as a catalyst for the renewal in Toronto, was scheduled to minister at Mott on Sunday. He invited those with back problems and other ailments to come up to the front. As a large clump of people crowded to the side of the front platform, Randy simply asked them to put their hands on the area of pain.

Angeles put her hands on what was left of her devastated disks. To her amazement, she recalls "Heat came out of my hands, my legs shook! I closed my eyes and the Lord showed me a picture of my back. It was perfect!"

She placed her hands on her stomach for other ailments, and the heat increased. She fell to the floor under the power of the Holy Spirit. Moments later when she got up, she realized that Jesus had healed her.

Wanting to be sure, she kept her appointment a week later with the new chiropractor. Immediately, he knew something had happened. As he examined her, it became evident that the healing was real. In his report, he states, "I cannot totally explain why this patient...became totally clear. She is convinced that her back was totally healed by Jesus' will and I have found nothing in my record to contradict the things she is telling me."

Such a miracle would be no surprise to Cindy Loong, who also found healing for her TMJ at Mott. Excerpts from her testimony recall the following from the November 1995 issue of *Harvest Times*:

I had been suffering from this complex dental disorder (TMJ or Temporomandibular Joint Disorder) for more than ten years. Many members of my family's church and denomination had been praying for me for more than two years. I had seen more than ten dentists, hoping to find a cure.

Our family, originally from China, has been conservative Baptist for three generations. My parents have been missionaries for many years. In general, we had not emphasized divine healing or other gifts of the Spirit. However, I decided it was time to check things out.

I attended the renewal meetings four times. Each time I requested prayer for my jaw, but it seemed like nothing happened. Meanwhile, my mother, Helen, was due to arrive from out of the country on Thursday, August 17th. The day she arrived, she decided to attend Mott.

And then it happened.

That evening, the guest speaker, Sean Smith, delivered a dynamic message. Towards the end, he said, "I have a feeling that God wants to do a great work of healing tonight." He then proceeded to call out several medical cases that needed attention.

The first case he described was, "There's a woman in the audience who has soreness in the left side of her mouth, in the gums, and she has had problems eating for quite a while..."

He went on to describe more details of my situation. There was no way he could have known anything about me!

In complete awe, I stepped out to the front with others behind me who were going to receive prayer for healing. During the prayer, I could sense my lower jaw move around several times. At the end of the prayer, I moved my jaw around as my dentist usually asks me to do at his clinic. There was no grating, which had been one of the symptoms of the TMJ.

Because of God's perfect timing, my mother was there to witness this miracle first hand. God received even greater glory as the news of this testimony reached across the country via my parents' mailing list.

The very next week, I visited my dentist, Dr. Ott. After examining my jaw with the usual tests, he concluded that the "membrane had indeed slipped back over the condyle, in between the bones," which I had been praying for all this time. In fact, my lower jaw had shifted so much that my lower front teeth no longer contacted the splint above. Dr. Ott was truly amazed and admitted that this was the first miracle case he had ever witnessed in his clinic.

I praise God for what He is doing and has done in my life. I thank Him for all His blessings and surprising me with the power of His Spirit.

To this day, God continues to heal people at Mott sovereignly; and I mean sovereignly—without anyone on the ministry team even praying for them!

An Explosive Healing

Jenni is just one example. She was partially deaf, having experienced significant hearing problems since she was young. She wore a hearing aid that helped her, but still it did not give her full hearing abilities.

While she was worshiping, her hearing aid exploded in her ear. She thought the hearing aid was malfunctioning, but she soon realized she was totally healed of her hearing problem. She went to have her hearing tested and gave me a copy of her test results for my files. Her hearing is now perfect. God in His love sovereignly touched her and she was healed.

Believing God for the Miraculous

I honestly can say I have witnessed more people healed in the first three and one-half years of this visitation than the previous 21 years of walking with the Lord. I believe it is only the beginning.

Cindy Jacobs prophesied the following in the October 1996 issue of her organization's *GI Newsletter:*

This is a crucial hour for My church when I desire to pour out My glory in a greater measure than has ever been seen.

Satan is trembling and working diligently to get you to doubt me because of the wave of glory and miracles I am getting ready to pour forth across the earth. Signs and wonders will come to the church, not just trickles, but in a flood: a flood of the miraculous. You will see the dead rise, the deaf hear, and the blind see. Once again the ambulances will bring the people to the church because I am the God of the impossible. Believe me. Declare war on unbelief and get ready to receive the flood of the miraculous that will sweep thousands of souls into the Kingdom.

I couldn't agree more. It is time for the Church to declare war on unbelief and believe God for the miraculous. It is time to believe for the sake of those who suffer, but even more so for the sake of those who are lost. Miracles, signs and wonders are one of God's most potent tools to reach the lost. The greatest miracle of all is still a soul coming to Christ.

I believe that we are in the beginning stages of the greatest harvest of souls the Church has ever seen. This visitation is about the Holy Spirit releasing the power to win the lost. It began to happen in the very early days of Harvest Rock Church.

MAKING IT REAL...PRACTICAL SUGGESTIONS

- Earnestly desire spiritual gifts such as healing and those gifts related to it, such as faith, working of miracles and the word of knowledge.
- Become equipped in the healing ministry by attending conferences and seminars.
- Receive prayer and impartation whenever possible from those who have the gift of healing.
- Read books such as C. Peter Wagner's *How to Have a Healing Ministry in Any Church* or John Wimber's *Power Evangelism* to build up your faith and give you understanding of the gift.
- Step out and start praying for people!

POWER EVANGELISM

―――――■―――――

The renewal services have brought a whole new perspective to me about the power of God to save souls. Akiko is only one reason I will never evangelize as I did before.

AN UNBELIEVER'S POWER ENCOUNTER

Akiko came reluctantly to one of our services. A young Japanese woman, she had been invited by another Japanese student. Her friend was studying at nearby Fuller Theological Seminary, and had himself experienced a powerful encounter with the Lord just days earlier. While visiting Mott Auditorium, he was filled with the Holy Spirit and speaking in tongues (see Acts 2:4)—much to his own surprise. He had previously enjoyed mocking charismatics, and he was the last person he would expect to become one!

When I first saw Akiko after the service, I remember asking her if she spoke English. "A little," she replied. I asked her if she wanted to accept Jesus into her heart. Hesitating briefly, she countered, "No, I cannot. My father is a Shinto. My mother is a Buddhist."

I told her I understood. Having visited Japan, and having many internationals as friends, I knew that the number of Christians in Japan is less than 1 percent. One reason is that a Japanese must readily conform to the norm of its society. Becoming a Christian is contrary to the norm.

In essence, it would mean having to renounce the family and the cultural heritage. The Japanese have a saying: "If a nail is sticking up, it has to be hammered down." A person cannot stick out differently from the rest. So when Akiko said she could not become a Christian because her parents were not, I understood.

I asked if I could pray a blessing upon her anyway, and she said yes. Although many Japanese may not receive Christ, they are some of the most polite people I know and they will usually welcome your prayers.

When I prayed, I simply asked the Holy Spirit to give a revelation of Jesus to Akiko (see Eph. 1:17). As soon as the words left my mouth, the Holy Spirit fell on her. She slumped to the floor, and remained there for 20 minutes.

I had seen many people fall under the Spirit's power before, but to the best of my knowledge, they were already Christians. I remember wondering, *Isn't this interesting. Here is a nonbelieving Japanese resting in the Spirit.*

Akiko rested for quite some time. After a while, I became concerned because she was still lying on the floor, and she hadn't moved an inch. I came back to her, got down on my knees and asked if she was okay. She nodded her head affirmatively.

"Akiko, did Jesus reveal Himself to you?" I asked.

She nodded her head up and down again.

"Would you like to invite Jesus into your heart and become a follower of Him?" I continued. She nodded yes!

I helped her up to a sitting position. We prayed the sinner's prayer, and Akiko became a beautiful Christian. Since then she has grown in her commitment to the Lord in spite of the opposition by her family.

The lesson I learned was that I could have talked to Akiko until I was blue in the face. I could have shared all my best apologetics about how Jesus is superior to Buddha. I could have spoken with great fervor and insight—but most likely it would not have changed her mind about Jesus.

Yes, she might have prayed a prayer with me because she felt pressured, or just to be polite, but I doubt she truly would have given her heart to the Lord. Yet when she experienced the love, the presence and the power of the Holy Spirit firsthand, her heart was opened and she responded with all the sincerity within her.

CHANGING MY EVANGELISM PHILOSOPHY

This experience has changed my whole philosophy of evangelism. Before, I would simply present the gospel and allow the person to either accept or reject Christ. Now, I know there is no comparison to allowing an unbeliever to first encounter the matchless reality of the Holy Spirit before I try to lead the person to the Lord.

This also gave me a whole new insight into "power evangelism," a term popularized by the late John Wimber. John, who led the Vineyard denomination, did much to better equip Christians to share the reality of the gospel, followed by signs and wonders, and not just the "facts" about salvation.

In short, power evangelism takes place when an unbeliever sees and experiences the power of God in a mighty way—such as through miracles or healings, along with a rational presentation of the gospel.[1] Peter Wagner unapologetically says, "Across the board, the most effective evangelism in today's world is accompanied by manifestations of supernatural power."[2] I personally believe that the primary expansion of Christianity in the Early Church came as a result of power evangelism. It is not new—just far more rare than it needs to be.

Although I love all kinds of evangelism and I admire anyone who is devoted to this great cause, I believe the most effective salvation we can demonstrate anywhere on the planet comes through this kind of a power encounter. There is no question in my mind that such demonstrations are the cutting edge of what the Holy Spirit is saying concerning evangelism. It is as old as the Bible. Again and again, we observe people believing in the gospel after experiencing signs and wonders. Just look at the book of Acts!

Spiritual scales are removed from the eyes of unbelievers as they experience or witness the power of God. Second Corinthians 4:4 says, "The god of this age has blinded the minds of unbelievers, so that they cannot see the light of the gospel." When they experience a healing or see a miracle such as took place in the city of Samaria (see Acts 8), however, their spiritual eyes are opened and great salvation occurs!

My problem was that I had narrowly relegated power evangelism to the limited number of people who directly see or experience such a miracle or healing. Now I was discovering that non-Christians could experience the presence and the power of the Holy Spirit in other ways that opened their hearts to the gospel just as greatly.

I found that all I had to do was to ask the Holy Spirit to touch them, or to reveal Jesus to them. The anointing did the rest.

BINDING THE POWER
OF DARKNESS

What happened this particular day was another wonderful illustration.

Two high school summer-exchange students—also from Japan—came to our Sunday church service. As practicing Buddhists, this was their first time in a Christian church. Their American host, a member of Harvest Rock Church, decided to bring them along to church.

I had an opportunity to meet the two young girls and their host before the service began. I encouraged the host to bring the students to the front of the church at the end of the service during our time of personal ministry. I knew that any encounter they could have with the Holy Spirit was likely to cause them to be more open to the gospel, and I didn't want them to miss this.

At the end of the service, I saw the host and the two girls coming toward me. Through Yoshi, a Japanese church member and interpreter, I asked if I could pray for them. They both nodded yes. I wasn't concerned that they might only be polite.

As I began to pray, the Holy Spirit started to fall on them. They both started to sway, one more so than the other. I began to discern some strong demonic hindrances, so I asked through Yoshi about their religious background. At this time I heard

■

"THE KINDNESS OF GOD LEADS US TO
REPENTANCE." WHAT BETTER WAY TO EXPERIENCE
THE KINDNESS OF GOD THAN TO FEEL IT!
SURELY IT IS BETTER FELT THAN TAUGHT!

from their own mouths that they were Buddhists.

Because Satan blinds the eyes of the unbelieving, I was led in this particular situation to bind the powers of darkness that were hindering these two from receiving Jesus (see Matt. 16:19; 18:18). Then I began to pray that God would reveal His love to each of them.

I clearly could see that they were now being mightily overshadowed by the presence of the Holy Spirit (see Luke 1:35; 9:34). I briefly proceeded to share with them how Jesus had died for them, and asked if they would like to receive Jesus into their hearts. They both said yes, and became Christians!

Although they didn't fall under the power of the Holy Spirit before the prayer of salvation as Akiko had, one fell after accepting Christ. As each one personally experienced the power and presence of the Holy Spirit, however, the gospel became real as they heard the explanation of salvation, and both of their hearts were turned to Christ!

SHARING THE TRUTH OF THE GOSPEL

I want to state emphatically that the truth of the gospel must be shared clearly in words as well, but I believe it can be better received after experiencing the power of the Holy Spirit.

My theory is that such a power encounter with the Lord pulls down the spiritual forces that are hindering the person from coming to Christ, and the love of God is revealed. Paul states that "the kindness of God leads us to repentance" (see Rom. 2:4). What better way to experience the kindness of God than to feel it! Surely it is better felt than taught!

Since the renewal started, I have seen more than 50 people in my church alone come to the Lord who would traditionally be considered difficult to reach—such as the Japanese. Yet by simply laying my hands on their heads and praying for the Holy Spirit to come and reveal Jesus, things changed.

POWER EVANGELISM IS GETTING THE JOB DONE

Without the power of the Holy Spirit, we can in no way reach the three billion people who have never heard the gospel. Around the world, power evangelism is getting the job done.

One of the most inspiring stories I have ever read illustrating the advancement of the kingdom of God through power evangelism is the story of Robert Kanyanja. The story is told by George Otis Jr. in his outstanding book *The Twilight Labyrinth*.

In December 1983, this young Ugandan evangelist was invited to hold an evangelistic crusade in the oppressed town of Soroti. After much prayer, fasting and spiritual warfare, the results were amazing. "The power of God swept across the crowd, dissolving tumors, opening blind eyes and restoring withered limbs. At least six cripples walked out of the meeting under their own power."[3]

As a result, a major church was established, called the Miracle Center. Robert shares what has happened since: "By the mid-1990s, the Miracle Center, our main church, was hosting about seven thousand on Sunday morning. And the numbers continue to grow. Two hundred and thirty-six branch fellowships were planted in this same period, and at least six dead people have been raised to life."[4]

LAUGHING REVIVAL

The toughest circumstances can be changed by praying for the Holy Spirit's touch—such as Lisa's. Lisa was particularly distant. She was a 15-year-old Korean-American teenager who grew up alongside gang-member friends in the Las Vegas area.

She had been shot at twice. One time she ducked at the last second, and a bullet flew right over her head. Her mother didn't know what to do with her, so she sent her to live with her aunt in Seattle, Washington.

I recall when her aunt shared with me in exasperation and desperation how out of control Lisa's life had become. She was rebellious, a crack addict and wasting away on drugs and gangster rap music. I told her aunt to bring her to my evening ministry appointment. That evening I was scheduled to speak to a small group of Korean Christians.

When Lisa came in, you couldn't miss her. She stood out like a sore thumb. There she was in her baggy, gang-looking clothes. A dark shadow seemed to veil her hardened face. She didn't look 15; she looked like a burned-out adult.

At least I knew one unbeliever was attending the meeting. I think she was the only non-Christian at this gathering. During my whole message, I was continually conscious of her. In all honesty, I was preaching to Lisa hoping she would respond to the altar call I would give at the end of the service.

I gave the altar call, but Lisa didn't respond. After the altar call, we had a ministry time. I began to pray for people to be filled with the Holy Spirit. People were falling to the ground as the Holy Spirit fell on them. They were "manifesting" or showing God's presence on them by shaking or trembling as well. I

was wondering what was going through Lisa's mind. I decided
to go to her.

After introducing myself and chatting for a moment, I simply asked Lisa if she would like to give her life to Jesus. She told

■

**MANY HAVE CALLED THIS RENEWAL THE
"LAUGHING REVIVAL" BECAUSE PEOPLE LAUGH
UNCONTROLLABLY WHEN THE HOLY SPIRIT
FILLS THEM WITH SUCH UNSPEAKABLE JOY.**

me she wasn't ready yet. I said I appreciated the honest answer,
but asked if she would mind if I prayed for her anyway.

"Do whatever you want," she said indifferently. She seemed
bored and ready to bolt at the earliest opportunity. Not wanting to crowd her or add to her discomfort, I stood several feet
away as I prayed.

"Jesus, please reveal to Lisa how much you love her," I asked
quietly.

As soon as I said those words, Lisa started to laugh. At first I
wondered if she was laughing at me or at what I had prayed. I
soon saw that she was trying not to laugh as she made a futile
effort to cover her mouth with her hands. That is when I knew
this laughter was the Holy Spirit flooding her!

Many have called this renewal the "laughing revival"
because people laugh uncontrollably when the Holy Spirit fills
them with such unspeakable joy. When I realized this was happening to Lisa, I said to her, "Don't fight the laughter. The Holy
Spirit is revealing Himself to you!"

At this point, I went near her to bless what the Father was
doing and to ask for more. As soon as I lifted my hands, she fell
to the floor speaking in tongues. This amazed me. I hadn't led
her to the Lord, nor had we prayed the sinner's prayer. In fact,

she had just told me she wasn't ready to come to Christ!

I asked the Lord to give me Scripture concerning what I was witnessing. Immediately, Acts 10 came to my mind. As Peter was preaching to the house of Cornelius, the Holy Spirit fell, and the members of the household all began to speak in tongues.

Apparently, God, who knows the hearts of people, must have known that Lisa changed her mind when she experienced that initial touch of the Spirit in laughter. She then was converted and filled with the Holy Spirit all at the same time!

Lisa stayed on the floor for almost two hours. She was still speaking in tongues and shaking under the power of the Spirit. Everyone had gone home except a few people, including Lisa and her aunt. I needed to be going, so I leaned over and told her it was time to go home.

"I can't move. I can't get up," she replied. "There are too many...too many!"

I thought she was saying she was seeing too many demons, and that I would have another late night staying to minister deliverance.

"There are too many what?" I queried.

"Too many faces!" she answered.

"Faces of whom?" I asked.

"Faces of my friends. Their faces have been flashing before me all night," came the reply.

Her answer hit me with tremendous force. Not only did God save her, fill her with His Spirit and give her a prayer language, but He also gave her the Spirit of intercession! For almost two hours, that is what Lisa had been doing. She was praying for her gang-member friends!

God gave me important insight from His heart that night: This next generation is so vital to Him, and intercession is such a key part of their revival that God wants to save and recruit young people on the spot just as He did Lisa. There is no time to lose as they cry out for their perishing friends!

Lisa stayed on the floor unable to move for the next eight hours. When I saw her the next day, I hardly recognized her.

She was radiant. She looked soft. She looked like a 15-year-old.
We baptized her, and to this day, she is a transformed young lady.

Power evangelism works. The key to this power is prayer, extraordinary prayer. This is another truth of renewal in which I found myself growing more than at any other time of my life.

MAKING IT REAL...PRACTICAL SUGGESTIONS

- Take the initiative to incorporate new methods of evangelism into the style to which you are accustomed. Learn about friendship or servant evangelism or power evangelism. Read books such as *Conspiracy of Kindness* by Steve Sjogren, or *Power Evangelism* by John Wimber and Kevin Springer.
- Practice prayer evangelism, or ask people to share their felt needs and then pray for them. Invite Jesus to reveal Himself to them as you pray.
- Consider initiating the Alpha Course in your area. This course began in England, and is perhaps the best evangelism tool for renewal churches. It brings together personal evangelism, servant evangelism, proclamation and power evangelism in a well-established format that is easy to sponsor in any church or group.

Notes

1. John Wimber and Kevin Springer, *Power Evangelism* (San Francisco: HarperSanFrancisco, 1986; 2nd revised and expanded edition, 1992), p. 35.
2. C. Peter Wagner, *The Third Wave of the Holy Spirit* (Ann Arbor, Mich.: Vine Books, Servant Publications, 1988), p. 87.
3. George Otis Jr , *The Twilight Labyrinth* (Grand Rapids: Chosen Books, 1997), p. 261.
4. Ibid., p. 295.

HOUSE OF PRAYER FOR ALL THE NATIONS

Billy Graham says there are three keys to his crusades: (1) Prayer, (2) Prayer, (3) Prayer.

John Wesley said, "Everything by prayer and nothing without it." I couldn't agree more.

All that has happened at the Mott Auditorium is a direct result of prayer. I actually have heard some say that the current renewal hit the world sovereignly without prayer. I understand why people might say this. The Toronto group, for example, was not having any unusual prayer sessions before the Holy Spirit fell on January 20, 1994. To my knowledge, neither did the Anaheim Vineyard.

I believe, however, the Holy Spirit always falls in answer to prayer. I agree with what one leader said: "There has never been a historic revival without extraordinary prayer." This current visitation is most likely a result of all the fervent prayers of the Body of Christ offered during the 1980s and early 1990s.

Although the Church as a whole did not see much fruit during that decade, one thing it did do was pray.

The same was true for us. At least we prayed, especially my friend Lou Engle.

AN INCOMPARABLE INTERCESSOR

My mentor and professor, Dr. Peter Wagner, once said if he were going to plant a church, the first person he would recruit would be an intercessor.

By God's grace, I did not need to recruit one. God had already joined me with Lou Engle, an incomparable intercessor. Lou is far more than a prayer warrior who oversees intercession in our church. He has been a loyal friend, confidant, partner and fellow pastor.

In fact, Lou has been a "Father Nash" to me. Father Nash was the man who traveled with Charles Finney and interceded while Finney preached. Often as I have led meetings and been the primary speaker, Lou has prayed. He reminds me of Frank Bartleman, a revivalist who gave himself to fasting and prayer during the Azusa Street Revival. I have never met anyone who embodied and personified prayer as does Lou Engle.

EXTRAORDINARY PRAYER

Jonathan Edwards said if you want to experience revival, there must be "explicit agreement, visible union and extraordinary prayer." A trail of such prayer pervades the accounts of what has happened at Harvest Rock Church. Or, as Alice Smith puts it, "Pray until something happens."[1]

When we began Harvest Rock Church, we started as a prayer meeting. When we heard from God to go into protracted renewal meetings, we began the first 21 days by praying and fasting.

That was the first time I had been on a 21-day liquid fast. We met 5 days a week for prayer, and in the evenings we had renewal meetings. It is hard to believe we have hosted the sec ond longest renewal meetings in the world, except for the Toronto movement, which is first. I firmly believe it is because we devote, dedicate and sustain the meetings through prayer.

CONTINUOUS PRAYER

A key development in the life of our church came in the fall of 1995.

The Lord began to impress upon Lou Engle that we should establish a Twenty-Four Hour House of Prayer for All Nations. For years, Lou wanted to establish this kind of sustained prayer, but the timing wasn't right. Now, the Lord was giving us permission to do so.

We held a meeting of hand-chosen intercessors and shared the vision of around-the-clock prayer at Mott. Each day had been divided into three-hour shifts from which intercessors could select. Their commitment was to one three-hour shift a week, during which time they could invite anyone they desired to join them in prayer.

Lou was also inspired to create a clear job description and outline of what needed to be covered during each shift.

A special room was devoted exclusively to the task, which contained a map of the world covering a full wall, thick carpet, kneeling rails, pillows and a variety of chairs. The shelves were dedicated to quality materials about prayer and world missions. New journals were placed in the room to cover current prayer requests and answers, record prophecies, revelations and dreams, and list the names of those involved in ministry from our midst around the world. A wide selection of praise and worship music and a small stereo completed the simple furnishings.

To inaugurate the prayer room, we decided to call our church to an extended time of praying and fasting for the first 40 days of 1996. During this time, Lou personally baptized that room by praying and fasting for 40 days. The last 10 days, he literally lived in the prayer room, praying without ceasing. He

home across the street only to shower and change
'r the 40 days were completed, the prayer shifts
...est, and continue to this day.

. uon't know where we would be as a church if the intercessors had not given of themselves in prayer. I want to thank every

■

RICK JOYNER WROTE OF HIS VISION OF
HEAVEN: THOSE CLOSEST TO THE THRONE OF
GOD [ARE] THOSE WHO GAVE THEMSELVES
TO INTERCESSION ON EARTH.

person who has been involved with our House of Prayer—and
others who so labor to build the kingdom of God throughout
the earth. I know you are doing a great work for the Lord, and
your reward will be abundant in heaven (see Matt. 6)!

As Rick Joyner wrote of his vision of heaven: Those closest
to the throne of God were those who gave themselves to intercession on earth. He described his vision in further detail: "As
I approached the Judgement Seat of Christ, those in the highest
ranks were also sitting on thrones that were all a part of His
throne...it seemed that faithful, praying women and mothers
occupied more thrones than any other single group."[2]

I believe this is so. God asks us to "give him no rest till he
establishes Jerusalem and makes her the praise of the earth"
(Isa. 62:7).

That is certainly our desire, and as the Lord continues to
grace us, we will not cease. The Moravians, unparalleled reform-
ers and catalysts of revival and missions centuries ago, held continuous prayer sessions for more than 100 years. We would like
to experience continuous prayer until the Lord returns.

The Bible tells us that the gospel of the Kingdom must be
preached to all the nations, "and then the end will come"

(Matt. 24:14). Until all the peoples of the world have been reached, we will continue to pray and fast around the clock. This is what we believe the Lord has asked of us.

Although not everyone is called to establish a Twenty-Four Hour House of Prayer, we can all do something. God has led many churches to sponsor a weekly all-night prayer meeting. The important thing is to do what you consider the Father is showing you in regard to prayer.

For more insight, you may wish to contact our ministry and ask for Lou's teaching about Atomic Power Through Prayer and Fasting. We would also be happy to give you more information about our House of Prayer.

FORTY DAYS OF PRAYING AND FASTING

Lou is the only one I know personally who has been on three 40-day fasts.

I jokingly say that I hired Lou to be on staff to do the fasting while I do the eating. Quite frankly, I hate to fast. In fact, I used to think I didn't need to fast. My wife, Sue, is another person who has given herself to prayer and fasting. I reasoned that between Sue and Lou's dedication, the whole church and I were covered, but I was wrong.

In the latter part of 1996, God began to confront me about an extended fast. Like many people, I had read Bill Bright's book about fasting, *The Coming Revival.* In it, Bright contends "the power of fasting as it relates to prayer is the spiritual atomic bomb of our moment in history to bring down the strongholds of evil, bring a great revival and spiritual awakening to America, and accelerate the fulfillment of the Great Commission."[3] The Lord began to speak to me that we as a pastoral staff should go on a 40-day fast together in 1997.

We had heard about the pastors and churches in Houston fasting the last 40 days of 1996, led by city leader, Doug Stringer, of Someone Cares Houston. (It must be God's doing to fast through Thanksgiving and Christmas!) John Arnott had shared with me that his church in Toronto was planning a corporate fast the first 40 days of 1997.

I also heard that some 50 pastors and their churches in Dallas were planning to do the same thing. We decided our fast would begin one week after Lent, and culminate 40 days later on Easter Sunday.

In January, I shared the idea with the church, noting that we were committed to the fast as a pastoral staff and anyone who so desired could join us. To my amazement, more than 600 people made a commitment to participate in the fast in some way. Many people went on a vegetable fast, others ate one meal a day, and so on. More than 65 people engaged in a liquid fast for the entire 40 days. I was one of them.

Initially, I had a hard time. I was used to drinking diet Coke, so the first three days I suffered caffeine withdrawal and experienced headaches and fatigue. The second week I started to dream of food almost nightly. I remember one dream. I had come home and I saw a bowl of rice and a plate of Korean barbecue on the table. The dream seemed so real I sat down and devoured the food. Then I realized I had broken my fast. I felt terrible. I felt like Esau who had given over his birthright for some measly food. Then I realized there was nothing I could do because I had already broken the fast, so I decided I should eat more. I had another helping. When I woke up, I realized it was only a dream. I was so grateful!

I think the dream motivated me and helped me not to break the fast even when I was tempted to do so. One practical note concerning the fast: I was losing more muscle mass than body fat. After 10 days, a physician in our church warned me to drink some liquid protein and to do some light exercise. That was vital advice for my health. Soon I began to lose body fat and not muscle. Even after the fast, I have been able to keep off most of the weight I lost and am still 15 pounds lighter than before the fast. So far, so good!

Of course, losing weight was not the main reason for the fast. My main goal was to grow in love—a prayer God is still answering in many wonderful ways and I will yet share with you in the pages of this book.

We concluded the 40 days of fasting by conducting a healing conference. Mahesh Chavda was invited to be with us. On Friday night, he led us in a "prayer watch," which is essentially an all-night prayer meeting.

Around three in the morning, a most unusual thing happened. A huge tree in front of the auditorium split in half—as if struck by lightning. It happened to be right in front of my

■

GOD WAS GIVING US A SIGN TO ENCOURAGE US

THAT WE WERE RIGHT ON TRACK THROUGH

OUR OBEDIENCE IN FASTING AND PRAYER.

parking place! There was no wind, no rain, no lightning, or any other natural cause for such an occurrence!

A person who was leaving the prayer meeting reported what had happened. When I shared it with Mahesh, he thought it was a sign that demonic strongholds at Mott were broken, and that we would see a greater release of the Holy Spirit. Mahesh had witnessed this kind of thing several times before during his crusades in Africa. He told us that many times God would break the spirit of witchcraft by splitting a tree, usually by lightning. Most often, that particular tree was known to the local witches as a power source. Whether that applies to this particular incident or not, I do believe God was giving us a sign to encourage us that we were right on track through our obedience in fasting and prayer.

THE FRUIT OF PRAYER

Most likely, none of us will know the full effect of our intercessions in this life until we get to heaven. We do, however, know of several things that happened in our city that we believe were influenced greatly by our prayers and that of many others.

A dramatic change of name for one public landmark is but one of them.

Here is Lou's account of what happened:

Protecting the original water source of Pasadena and Los Angeles is a dam bearing the name of Devil's Gate. My fellow intercessors and I sensed strongly that such a name literally brought a curse on the city. A 1947 local newspaper article said, "It's true Devil's Gate is named because of the resemblance of the rocks to his satanic majesty."

One night I awoke from a dream with these words spoken to me: "Go and pour the salt of your purity on it." I didn't know what this word pertained to at that moment, but prior to coming to Pasadena, the Lord had given me a word from the passage where Elisha poured salt into the water source of Jericho and healed the contaminated waters (2 Kings 2:19-22).

That morning in a prayer meeting, an intercessor in our church prayed that God would change the name of Devil's Gate. Then it struck me with much force to go and pour salt into the stream at Devil's Gate as an act of prophetic intercession—and ask the Lord to change the name, break the curse, and let the rivers of revival flow bringing fruitfulness to the Los Angeles Valley.

We took our Greater Pasadena for Christ intercession team to the dam and did precisely that. At that time, Southern California had been experiencing a severe drought of five years duration. I know thousands of other Californians were praying for rain as well, but God encouraged us when eight days later it began to rain. The rains were so heavy the newspapers called it a "Miracle March." It was astonishing. We pondered this. Could it be a sign of renewal and revival—first the natural, then the spiritual?

However, for two years, the name of the dam remained

the same. One of our intercessors went to God to inquire again. He spoke to her that the name would be changed, and it would be an Indian name.

Soon after, a *Los Angeles Times* newspaper article added to our excitement of answered prayer when it spoke of a name change for the dam:

> Hahamongna—That's the name the Gabrielinos (early Pasadena Indians) gave to what now is known as "Devil's Gate," the 250-acre area at the north end of the Arroyo Seco...The English-language translation is "Flowing Waters: Fruitful Valley." Nearly everyone agrees that Hahamongna will be a more appropriate name for this long-neglected community asset after it is restored to its natural state....

Flowing rivers and a fruitful valley—that is our intercession now, and what has begun since the outpouring began in 1994.

Another major turnaround we witnessed in our city was the repentance and conversion of a major cult. Many people have no doubt heard of the Worldwide Church of God (WWCG), or its magazine, *The Plain Truth*.

In the early days of their being in Pasadena, we believed they were a major demonic stronghold in our city, and we repeatedly prayed and lifted them up. I am not saying we were the reason the WWCG changed, but we may have played a part.

God had been working on the organization for quite some time. I know many former members who had become Christians and were fervently interceding for WWCG. I do believe, however, the many collective prayers, including ours, were responsible for the change.

I remember Jack Hayford saying, "To my knowledge, never has a cult turned around so dramatically in the history of Christianity." Today, the WWCG is a member of the National Association of Evangelicals. I now know many of the leaders personally, including Joseph Tkach, the president of the WWCG. I honestly can say they are true brothers in Christ.

If God can bring down the walls of deception of the WWCG through the prayers of the saints, then we need to be earnest in faith and prayer that the scales of deception also fall from groups such as the Mormons and the Muslims.

PERSEVERING IN PRAYER

I am ever so grateful about what the Lord has done in bringing renewal to our city. Yet the temptation is not to be as fervent in prayer because things seem to be happening sovereignly.

We have learned that when God does pour out His unmerited grace, we should give ourselves to prayer as never before (see 1 Thess. 5:17). In addition, we have "not yet arrived." Yes, we are experiencing renewal, but it is not the same as the revival found in the book of Acts. We are not yet seeing multitudes swept into the Kingdom. I believe that renewal is part of revival, but it is the early stage when believers can be refreshed and renewed. A true historic revival, however, includes a great harvest and a reformation of society. As Alice Smith says in her book *Beyond the Veil*, "Burning, believing, prevailing, persuading, persevering, intimate prayer always precedes a move of God."[4]

To this end we continue to labor, pray and believe! We must press forth until He truly makes His people a praise on the earth!

MAKING IT REAL...PRACTICAL SUGGESTIONS

- Be enriched through the wealth of books and tapes now available about prayer.
- Books such as *The Lost Art of Intercession* by Jim Goll, *Intercessory Prayer* by Dutch Sheets, *Beyond the Veil* by Alice Smith, or any of the many great books by C. Peter Wagner are especially helpful.
- Be part of a prayer meeting even if only two or three are gathered.

- Attend a corporate prayer meeting regularly.
- Make it your aim to pray for a move of God in your life and that of your church and city, and don't neglect fervent, continual, personal prayer.
- Pray for your *oikos* list, which consists of your friends and relatives who live near the church.
- Practice fasting, and consider going on an extended fast. Be informed and inspired for an extended fast by reading Bill Bright's *The Coming Revival*.

Notes
1. Alice Smith, *Beyond the Veil* (Ventura, Calif.: Renew Books, 1997), p. 39.
2. Rick Joyner, *The Final Quest* (New Kensington, Pa.: Whitaker House, 1996), p. 116-117.
3. Bill Bright, *The Coming Revival* (Orlando, Fla.: NewLife Publications, 1995), p. 16.
4. Smith, *Beyond the Veil*, p. 22.

A NEW SPIRIT OF UNITY

Although I experienced renewal in 1994, many seeds had been planted before that time. One remarkable venture was a trip to Argentina in 1991. That single trip radically changed my view of myself and Christianity—and helped pave the way for the move of God that would come to Pasadena three years later.

I had heard about the revival in South America during my class taught by Dr. C. Peter Wagner at Fuller Seminary. My friend and mentor Peter also told of an upcoming fall conference in Argentina hosted by Ed Silvoso. Ed is an internationally known speaker and author, and a leader in the Argentine revival. The roster of speakers was unbelievable. I knew I had to go.

Besides, Lou Engle and I had always said that if revival ever erupted anywhere in the world, we would go and see it. We both agreed that had we lived during the great Azusa Street Revival in Los Angeles at the turn of the century, we would have done anything to go there. Because we were not around in 1906, we were not about to miss this opportunity!

CONFRONTING PRIDE
AND ARROGANCE IN ARGENTINA

The revival combined with the special conference seemed to make the fall of 1991 a perfect time to visit Argentina. The larger church movement I was a part of then graciously allowed me to go and represent the group, and our local church covered Lou's expenses. Lou and I soon found ourselves en route to attend the first Harvest Evangelism Conference in Buenos Aires.

The conference had not even officially begun when the Holy Spirit began convicting me of my sins of sectarianism and superiority. I had joined some 100 American delegates for a preconference meeting with Ed Silvoso. We enjoyed an authentic barbecue at an Argentine ranch, and gathered afterward to partake of the Lord's Supper.

As Ed led us in sharing communion, he spoke passionately about the unity of the Body of Christ. He lucidly conveyed that regardless of denominational backgrounds, God only saw one Church. To demonstrate this oneness, he asked us all to come together in one large huddle and wrap our arms around the people near us.

We huddled like a huge ball of people crowding toward the middle and toward each other. I can't really describe what happened next, but the contrast between the sense of unity I felt at that moment and my inability to see the Church as one simply broke me. I started to cry uncontrollably. God was convicting me of legalism and sectarianism in a big way; and it was only the beginning.

I wept throughout the conference. Without exaggerating, I think I cried more during this week than any other week in my life. During the meetings, Ed Silvoso spoke again about the unity of the Church. Again I wept.

Joe Aldrich, one of the leaders of the Prayer Summits in the Northwest United States, spoke of the unity he witnesses at their events. "We simply come together and pray and worship," he explained. "We have no other agenda. No one is scheduled to speak or teach, we simply come together and forget about our denominational background, or the size of our churches. We simply come as brothers."

"By the end of the three days together," Joe continued, "there is much confession of competition, jealousies, disunity and sectarianism."

As Joe was sharing, I began to weep where I sat as the Lord convicted me of the very same things these pastors confessed to each other at their summits. I repented for comparing our

■

WE THOUGHT WE WERE "THE CUTTING EDGE" OF WHAT GOD WAS DOING BECAUSE WE WERE "SPIRIT-FILLED"...AND THOUGHT OUR "NEW WINESKIN" OR PHILOSOPHY OF MINISTRY WAS TRULY "IT."

church with others and for not really praying for or blessing others. I asked forgiveness for my own sectarian heart, and for being competitive and jealous.

If I had heard the same messages elsewhere, I doubt that it would have struck me the same. The presence of God was so strong in Argentina that these simple words about unity exploded with conviction in my heart. Perhaps just being away from my own city and "territory" made a difference.

As Ed Silvoso wisely observes in his book *That None Should Perish*, "Historically, pastors and leaders have always come together to do something (a crusade, a seminar, etc.) rather than to become someone in Christ. The problem with program-centered unity is that once the program is completed, the 'unity' evaporates. What I am describing here is radically different. It is unity in Christ."[1] During these meetings in Argentina, God was beginning to show me what this really meant.

I knew I was making a scene by crying at the time, but I could not hold back my tears. A few nights later, Lou and I compared notes and realized we were both experiencing major dealings with God. We stayed up till 2:30 that morning crying out to the Lord and repenting of all He was showing us. We realized we had never done anything to reach out to the rest of the Body of Christ in our city or anywhere else I had served as pastor.

Sadly, we thought we were "the cutting edge" of what God was doing because we were "Spirit-filled" and had "the revelation" that He was restoring His Church. We had been so sure others were missing out on God's best, and thought our "new wineskin" or philosophy of ministry was truly "it."

By the time we prayed and confronted our pride and arrogance, our legalism and sectarianism, the night was far gone!

The weeping continued when we took a break during the conference to visit a city influenced by revival: the city called Resistencia. The pastors from that city shared how the Lord prepared them for revival by bringing unity to the pastors. For three years, 65 out of some 75 evangelical pastors in their city met every week for prayer.

They would pray for the success of the other churches represented in that room. They did more than pray. When a fellow pastor was devastated because part of his church building had burned down, the other pastors came and held an old-fashioned "barn raising"—Argentine style!

Then, after three years, they invited Carlos Annacondia to conduct a citywide crusade. If I remember correctly, some 50,000 came to Christ in that 40-day period.

As they were sharing this wonderful news, I began to weep again at my own selfishness in the way I related to other churches. I began to see that we will never have historic revival in any city without unity among its pastors. I determined right then and there that I would not only change by God's grace, but that I would also do anything I could to bring forth fruit of that repentance in my city of Pasadena when I returned.

112

BEGINNINGS OF UNITY

I was obsessed with the desire to implement unity in Pasadena. On the flight back from Argentina, I preached to every Christian I could reach on the plane about the importance of unity—as if they had not heard the same message as I at the conference. Nevertheless, my heart was so filled that I had to speak from its abundance.

When I returned to Pasadena, I wanted to meet any pastor who would be willing to meet with me. I found out that a city-wide prayer meeting had been scheduled the very week I returned. It was a "Concerts of Prayer" event, fashioned by David Bryant, and was being held in cities across the United States.[2]

Although I had never attended one of these meetings before, I was committed to go now. I wanted to participate in anything that had to do with the church at large in the area.

As it turns out, it seemed providential that I went to the meeting. That summer, several new pastors had moved to Pasadena to start their new church positions. This particular prayer meeting was dedicated to welcoming and praying for them. Thus, many ministers who normally would not attend such a meeting also came.

One of the pastors who attended regularly knew I had gone to Argentina, and asked me if I would share a brief testimony of what had happened while I was there. As he asked me, I sensed God was orchestrating a divine opportunity for me to repent of my sectarian ways in front of my fellow brothers in Pasadena.

"Argentina changed my life," I began. "Truly, revival is taking place there. Revival can take place here as well, if we will allow God to reveal our sins and ask Him to truly forgive us. God convicted me of my sins in Argentina. He convicted me that I have not loved you, my fellow pastors of this city. He has convicted me of my pride, my selfishness and how sectarian I have been. Will you please forgive me?" I uttered.

After speaking those words I sat down. One of the pastors stood up and said, "I think we need to respond to our brother. We forgive you, Ché."

I was grateful for what the Lord had done, but I was still not satisfied as I left the meeting. Something else seemed to be stirring in my spirit.

That Sunday, I shared with our congregation what the Lord had done in my life in Argentina. I also shared that I felt led to collect a spontaneous second offering to give to the various churches in the city.

We collected more than eight thousand dollars, which was a large sum for a second offering at Abundant Life Community Church. The elders gave me liberty to divide the amount into five hundred- to one thousand-dollar increments for gifts to various pastors and churches in the city.

I tried to be led by the Holy Spirit in distributing the money. My goal was to go to the various churches representing different denominations and ethnic groups. We gave a thousand dollars to Lake Avenue Congregational Church, as they were in the midst of a massive building project. We gave a thousand to Confirmed Word Faith Center, an African-American church in the city. We also gave a thousand dollars to Ralph Winter and the U.S. Center for World Mission, an evangelical parachurch organization that is very much a part of the church scene in Pasadena.

Some of the pastors I met with were surprised, some even shocked, as I gave them a check. Although the amounts were not huge, I could sense the walls between the churches were slowly coming down in our city.

MARCH FOR JESUS

The week after I returned from Argentina, Peter Wagner spoke to me about going to Texas for a "March for Jesus" planning meeting. He believed I had received an impartation in Argentina and I was the person who could best represent our city in beginning a local march.

Up till that time, the march had been highly successful in England as a show of Christian support for our shared faith and love in Jesus, but not much had happened with it in the United States.

Now Roger and Faith Forster and Graham Kendrick, leaders of the march, were coming to Texas for a national planning meeting.

I was somewhat reluctant to go because I had already been out of the country for 10 days, and only a week remained before the conference began in Texas. Yet I was riding on a passion to have our city unified, and the march seemed as though it would be a great way to begin. I agreed to go.

The leaders of the international march wanted to schedule the first event in the spring of 1992, less than six months away. Those who attended this historic convocation were asked to return to their cities and quickly organize the event. To be honest, I thought I was in over my head.

I was not a recognized leader in Pasadena and, in fact, had not related well to others in the city. I knew the only way for the march to be successful in Pasadena would be to have the involvement of the evangelical churches. Our demographics are such that the significant churches are not Pentecostal or charismatic, but more traditional evangelical.

When I returned from the Texas strategy session, I received a vote of confidence from Peter Wagner to follow through on the march. Yet I knew I needed far more than Peter's support. I quickly called the pastors of the seven largest evangelical churches in Pasadena, and simply invited them to have lunch at my expense at the best Chinese restaurant in town. It is amazing how good food will surface some of the busiest pastors—everyone I invited came!

After a delicious meal, I shared the vision of March for Jesus. I told them frankly that unless they would commit their support to the event, we could not have a march in Pasadena. I also told them I would be happy to serve in any capacity, but if they did not want a march, then I did not want one either.

One of the pastors asked, "So Ché, do you want a response now?"

"Yes," I replied. "The March for Jesus is less than six months away. The only way we can get ready in time is if I can get your commitment today." One by one, every single pastor affirmed his commitment as I made eye contact with each man around the table. The March for Jesus was on in Pasadena!

In my opinion, the 1992 march was a huge success in Pasadena. Three thousand people were involved. Some other marches around the country had a larger attendance, but most people who participated were charismatic. The Pasadena march comprised mainly evangelicals from established churches such as Lake Avenue Congregational Church and Pasadena Nazarene. More importantly, churches were coming together under the simple banner of worshiping and loving Jesus.

Helping as chairperson of the Pasadena March soon opened the door for me to serve on the national board of March for Jesus America. It was a privilege to fly to Austin, Texas, to meet and fellowship with godly people and national leaders such as Tom and Theresa Pelton and Don Finto, just to mention a few.

116 A greater door to open in my own backyard would be my involvement with Pastor Jack Hayford and "Love Los Angeles" (Love L.A.).

LOVE L.A.

Jack had invited around 75 pastors for a pre-Love L.A. breakfast meeting, and somehow I was invited.

Love L.A. was established by Jack Hayford, the senior pastor of The Church On The Way, the eight-thousand-member church in Van Nuys, California, and by Lloyd Ogilvie, then senior pastor of Hollywood Presbyterian Church and now the Chaplain of the United States Senate.

Intended as a pastors' prayer meeting, Love L.A. is held three to four times a year. Anywhere from 200 to 600 pastors gather to simply love Los Angeles through their prayers.

After this particular breakfast, held at The Church On The Way, Jack was mingling with people, and I approached him to offer my thanks for the wonderful work he was doing for our city. One thing led to another, and he asked me if I had some extra time to join him in his office. I could not believe Jack Hayford was inviting me to his office!

He said good-bye to a few other pastors and then he invited me upstairs. We sat down and began to talk. I began to share with him how the Lord had changed my life in Argentina, and how I was committed to doing what I could to effect unity in our city. Jack was visibly moved when I told him about the offering I had taken to assist some of the pastors in Pasadena.

"Ché, we have been looking for pastors like you to be a part of the leadership core of Love L.A. You not only have a passion for unity, but you are also Asian. We need more Asians involved in Love L.A. How would you like to be part of the servant leadership team with Lloyd and me?" he queried.

I could hardly believe what I was hearing. I was so stunned by the invitation that I hardly knew what to say. Of course, I told him that it would be an honor. I really did not realize what I was getting into until a few months later when I was invited to have lunch with the leaders of Love L.A.

The leaders during that time were Jack Hayford; Lloyd Ogilvie; Bishop Charles Blake, a pastor of the fourteen-thousand member Church of God in Christ in America, the largest of its kind; and Ken Ulmer, a bishop in a Charismatic Baptist denomination, another megachurch pastor.

As I sat there, I was saying to myself, *What is wrong with this picture? What am I doing here with all these great and famous pastors of megachurches?* Nevertheless, I knew God had placed me there. It was a privilege to be part of this group of leaders.

Each of these men accepted me as a friend and fellow pastor. I was honored when Lloyd asked me to share at his retirement service when he accepted the position of Chaplain of the United States Senate, but one of the greatest honors would be the opportunity to develop a wonderful mentoring and friendship relationship with Jack Hayford.

What is more, fulfilling the fruit and purpose of the Love L.A. outreach—as well as what I had learned on my trip to Argentina—contributed to another crucial element to affect Pasadena. It inspired me to initiate a weekly gathering of city pastors to meet together in prayer. This group eventually became the pastors who would cohost the protracted renewal meetings with me in the city. I have no doubt that this foundational unity served as a vital springboard for what God has been doing in Pasadena.

RACIAL RECONCILIATION

The riots of 1992, sparked by the brutal beating of Rodney King, brought the pastors of Love L.A. to an emergency prayer meeting at the Hollywood Presbyterian Church just after the riots.

The riots devastated Los Angeles, causing almost one billion

■

I WAS SEEING FOR THE FIRST TIME THE VERY

MAN GOD HAD SHOWN ME IN A VISION IN 1982.

RIGHT IN FRONT OF MY EYES WAS THE BLACK

MAN GOD HAD USED TO BID ME TO COME TO

LOS ANGELES SO MANY YEARS BEFORE.

dollars in damage. Almost half of that was in Korea Town. Tension between the Korean community and the African-American community had been ongoing. Newly arrived Koreans would buy up any business in South Central L.A., where businesses were more affordable. Instead of giving back to the community by hiring African-Americans, they would put their own families to work in order to save money.

The perception was that the Koreans were taking from the Black community and not giving back anything in return. The problem was compounded by the fact that many of the Koreans were afraid of the Blacks, and many African-Americans could sense the fear and the rejection from the Koreans.

Tension grew from bad to worse when Latasha Harlins, a teenager, was shot to death by a Korean business owner for allegedly stealing from the store. The conflict was caught on surveillance cameras on location and the whole nation soon became aware of the tension between the African-Americans and the Koreans in Los Angeles. It was no wonder that after the Rodney King beating incident the Koreans were targeted during the riots that erupted after the first trial.

We were all numb as we gathered as pastors to pray over our city that Tuesday afternoon. One by one, pastors came up to the mike to repent of racism. Then a large African-American man came up to the microphone, and instead of praying, he began to share his pain.

I immediately began to sob uncontrollably. It was not so much because of what this pastor was sharing, but because I was seeing for the first time the very man God had shown me in a vision in 1982. Right in front of my eyes was the Black man God had used to bid me to come to Los Angeles so many years before.

For years I had wondered why I was summoned to the West Coast by an African-American, but now it was all beginning to make sense.

I immediately began to realize that before racial reconciliation between the Koreans and Blacks in Los Angeles can occur, racial reconciliation and unity among the Korean Christians and Black Christians must take place.

Judgment always begins with "the family of God" (1 Pet. 4:17). As a Korean Christian, I had to do whatever I could to help bring healing between the two races.

At a later meeting with the leaders of Love L.A., I asked Jack Hayford if we could sponsor a reconciliation lunch between the Korean pastors and the African-American pastors. Jack and the leadership gave their total support and put me in charge of organizing it. It took almost a year for the meeting to come together, but God helped in a mighty way.

I began by contacting some of the key Korean pastors in the city. The main person I hoped to involve was Dr. Hee Min Park, the pastor of Young Nak Presbyterian Church, the largest Korean church in Los Angeles and in all of the United States. He agreed to come, and also invited other key Korean leaders.

Of course, Bishop Charles Blake would participate not only as a leader of Love L.A., but also as a representative of the largest Black church in Los Angeles. Other leading African-American pastors also attended at his invitation.

No one in the media knew this particular luncheon took place, but I believe it was historic. Something powerful took place that day in Los Angeles as Charles Blake stood up first and asked the Korean pastors for forgiveness for the damage done to Korea Town and the racism shown by the Black community. Then Dr. Park asked the African-American pastors for forgiveness for the racism of the Korean community. Jack Hayford and Lloyd Ogilvie were there to witness the whole event.

As with many things we do in obedience during our life of faith, only God knows the full significance of that meeting. I can't help but believe it was another step toward revival in our city, and that such a display of humility and unity would do the same for any location on the globe.

MAKING IT REAL...PRACTICAL SUGGESTIONS

- Repent of any sectarian spirit, or superiority or divisive mind-set.
- Be part of something larger than your church, such as a citywide or nationwide March for Jesus, or citywide prayer or worship gatherings.
- Cultivate a relationship with someone who is of another church.
- Cultivate relationships with those of another culture, color and background.

Notes
1. Ed Silvoso, *That None Should Perish* (Ventura, Calif.: Regal Books, 1994), p. 222.
2. David Bryant, *The Hope at Hand* (Grand Rapids: Baker Books, 1995).

TURNING THE HEARTS OF THE FATHERS TO THE CHILDREN

—————■—————

Like revival, true renewal brings permanent and wonderful change in the lives of those who experience it. Little did I know that perhaps the greatest change—the call to wholeness and holiness—could come through the love and laughter the Father is pouring out in this move.

The truth is that inside every believer is a desire to be holy in walking with the Lord. Yet all of us struggle greatly in our quest for victory over sin. Granted, holiness is a process—a truth that should set us free and release us from the condemnation that totally undermines our efforts. Wonderfully, however, I have grasped and experienced truths in this renewal that have enabled me to leap forward with tremendous strides in my personal endeavors toward this goal.

The greatest revelation I have received is that holiness has everything to do with love. We cannot be holy without first receiving His love. Again, it is God's initiative toward us—even as was our salvation.

God promises in Ezekiel 11:19,20, "I will give them an undivided heart and put a new spirit in them; I will remove from them their heart of stone and give them a heart of flesh. Then they will follow my decrees and be careful to keep my laws."

■

> TRUE HOLINESS AND VICTORY OVER SIN
> WILL NOT TAKE PLACE WITHOUT LOVE AS THE
> MOTIVATING FACTOR. FOR ONLY THEN IS
> OUR SURRENDER COMPLETE.

We cannot walk in obedience to His decrees without first having the stones removed from our hearts, and then receive more of His Spirit. This takes place when a person becomes a Christian, but I believe it is also a progressive experience in the believer's life. As God continues to remove the heart of stone and give us His Spirit, we move ahead on the pathway to holiness.

How God removes the heart of stone is through repentance. Repenting and receiving God's forgiveness softens us—for those who are forgiven much, love much (see Luke 7:47). The ability to repent is itself rooted in love, however, and again, God's initiative toward us.

In love and kindness God reveals our sins, and then from a heart of love, we respond by repenting. Although many may repent because of fear or feigned obedience, there is no greater or lasting repentance than that initiated through God's love. That is why Paul establishes the love of God in the first 11 chapters of Romans and then tells us in Romans 12:1: "In view of God's mercy, to offer your bodies as living sacrifices, holy and pleasing to God."

True holiness and victory over sin will not take place without love as the motivating factor. For only then is our surrender complete.

Renewal has brought just this kind of redemptive love into my life and that of countless others. God has lovingly revealed sins in my life and then poured out His Spirit in a way that has helped me overcome the very root and origin of these sins. Sins that were deeply ingrained have fallen off like shackles from a slave. I have never felt so free in my life. It feels as though, even after walking 20 years with the Lord, I am being born again and again.

People who have criticized this renewal say, "Where is the repentance?" "What is the laughter all about?" "Revival is not about laughter, but about repentance."

What many people do not realize is that in this move more true repentance has been taking place inside most people than at any other time in their walk with Jesus. I know this is true in my own life. Nothing changes us like the love of God. The goodness of God does lead to repentance (see Rom. 2:4). As Paul encouraged us in 1 Corinthians 12:31, love is indeed "a more excellent way" *(NKJV)*.

BITTER ROOTS

It was early October 1994, and my first trip to Toronto. I could sense the air of excitement as thousands flew to join the Toronto Christian Fellowship for the first "Catch the Fire Conference."

Lou Engle and I had been champing at the bit to go to Canada since the beginning of the year. We had heard months prior that an unusual move of the Holy Spirit was taking place there. Of course, we were radically touched at the Vineyard Conference in Anaheim, but we knew quickly, as did the world, that Toronto was the new "Azusa Street" for this wave of the Holy Spirit.

Indeed, thousands had already flocked to Toronto. Lou and I had been so consumed with starting a new church that we had not yet been able to visit this new "Mecca" of revival.

Now we were finally on our way. My first encounter was a bit offbeat, and not quite what I had expected from the image

I had held in my mind of the outpouring. It was a meeting before the conference officially began, and we were packed like sardines into the original fellowship building, which seats 500 at most. It seemed to me that the most memorable feature of that event was my discomfort.

The tone of what God was doing in my life subtly but vitally changed as the conference got under way at the nearby Constellation Hotel.

As Lou and I arrived, we were greeted by several people who had also come to Toronto from our church. Two of them, fellow Koreans Mike Park and David Kim, joined me in finding seats very close to the front. That was a miracle in itself as more than three thousand people were present.

I do not remember who spoke that night; most likely it was John Arnott. I do not remember what was said. I do remember, however, what happened to me during the ministry time because it changed my life forever.

When it came time for people to come forward to receive personal ministry, I almost ran. My friends Mike and David had the same hunger. For those not familiar with the style of ministry in Toronto and in Pasadena, lines are clearly marked on the floor of the meeting place so that people may assemble in an orderly fashion and wait on the Lord.

The three of us ended up close to each other on the first row. Having been so powerfully touched by the tangible presence of God in Anaheim and knowing about the joy and manifestations spreading from Toronto, my only goal was to get blasted by the Holy Spirit. I wanted all the manifestations and more. I was so revived in January with the dose I had at the Vineyard Conference that I had to have more. I also wanted enough to bring back a fresh anointing to Harvest Rock Church.

When a member of the ministry team came up to me and started to pray, I felt a gentle presence of the Holy Spirit and went down on the carpet of the hotel meeting room. I could hear both Mike and David laughing as they hit the floor powerfully. Frankly, I was envious. I wanted the laughter, but I felt almost nothing. As I lay there, I asked the Lord to show me what He wanted me to receive that night.

Immediately, God began to show me bitterness in my heart toward a particular brother in the Lord. The Holy Spirit's conviction hit me so hard that I began to weep at the sinfulness of my heart. I lay there sobbing and repenting while my friends were engulfed in laughter and holy joy.

That night, God began to show me hurts I had suppressed and how I had denied they even existed instead of confronting them. Because the hurts were real, they developed into the "bitter roots" of which the Bible speaks in Hebrews 12:15.

Having the loving presence of the Holy Spirit ministering to me that night, I could now face the pain that was too deep to acknowledge in everyday circumstances. Though it would be difficult to walk it through to a resolution, there was now a presence, a leading and a grace about the whole situation that I had never before experienced.

In the months ahead, I was able to resolve the bitterness toward the particular brother and, as we had opportunity to meet together, ask for his forgiveness for wrongs I had done to him. This progress unearthed the foundation of a deeper wound God wanted to heal in my life.

BITTER ROOTS TOWARD MY FATHER

The reason I was bitter toward this brother was that I felt rejected by him. I came to understand that this sensitivity to rejection really went back to the feelings of rejection I experienced from my dad.

Before I tell you what happened, please let me share with you a few important things about my dad. His name is Byung Kook Ahn. My father is also a pastor, and truly a great man of God. I say that not just because I am his son, but those who know him recognize it also. He is a pastor who is highly respected on a national level in the Korean community both in the United States and in Korea.

He was elected as the president of his church's denomination twice. He has spoken in some of the largest churches in Korea, including Full Gospel Central Church, pastored by Yonggi Cho. He also held a revival service at Kwang Lin, the largest Methodist church in the world, which has 70,000 members and is pastored by Sun Do Kim. He has authored several books. He was also the first Korean Baptist pastor (Southern Baptist affiliate) in North America. More important, he is a man of character who demonstrates a love and a passion for Jesus.

I can honestly say that my dad is one of the kindest, most generous and gracious men I know. I have tremendous respect for him and am grateful for all the sacrifices he made for us as a father and as a pastor. I have a deep love for him. Today, our relationship has never been better—but it was not always that way.

When I was only two, my father left my mother, my four-year-old sister, Chung-Hae, and me behind in Korea so he could accept a pastoral position in the Washington, D.C. area. The year was 1958.

Obviously, my father wanted his family to fly to Washington with him, but we were not granted a visa. He went on alone ahead of us, believing for a quick resolution to a difficult separation. It would be more than two years before we were released to join him in the United States.

During those two formative years, I missed my father greatly. I remember finally getting off the plane and eagerly running up to the man my mother pointed out to me as my dad. He picked me up. All I could say was, "I know that you're my father, but you don't look like my father!"

It is amazing the things you remember after all the years that have passed. During the two-year separation when I was so young, I really had little opportunity to ever know my father and in fact had forgotten what he looked like.

As my childhood progressed, I do not remember spending much time with my dad. He was extremely busy pastoring and had to work a second job as a dental technician to support his family.

Working two full-time jobs, pastoring a church and taking

care of a family in a new country, my father was experiencing enormous stress. His motive for coming to the United States was to leave a war-torn country and to provide a good education and future for his family. My sister, Chung-Hae, was an excellent student. I was a slow learner, though, and struggled in school. When I brought home mediocre report cards, I was physically punished by my father for not trying harder.

It was not long before I resented my father. I felt rejected by him. The rejection led to my looking for acceptance elsewhere, and I found it among my friends at school. I was always popular and I was always a leader (as far as I can remember). I guess God had given me those leadership qualities from birth. However, I soon led my friends into lawlessness and rebellion. Drinking alcohol and taking drugs became a regular habit.

I do not blame my father for getting upset with me for being rebellious, because I was. Unfortunately, the rebellion led to more physical punishments and more feelings of rejection and resentment.

When I came to Christ, I tried to work through much of the pain from those turbulent preconversion years. I remember going to a Bill Gothard "Basic Institute in Youth Conflicts" Ministry Conference and coming home and asking my father and my mother to forgive me for all the pain I had caused them. They gladly forgave me, but I never confronted my father for the pain he had caused me.

While on the floor in Toronto, God began to reveal an entire arena of bitterness in my heart connected to the hurts I still carried from my father. I realized I needed to talk to my father, but I did not have the courage to initiate the subject. Finally, the right opportunity came when my father and mother flew to Pasadena for my brother Chae-Woo's wedding in November 1996.

MY MALACHI 4:6 EXPERIENCE

I was very nervous throughout the day I had planned to talk with my father. I was not sure how I could communicate to him the hurts I had carried for 24 years. Just asking him to meet with me took all the nerve I could muster. Realizing how difficult it was to communicate with him showed me how deep and serious the hurts were in my life.

"Dad, can I talk with you privately?" I asked.

"Sure, son. Why don't you drive me to the hotel and we can talk on the way?" he replied.

I could not get into the conversation as we drove to the Pasadena Hilton. I wanted to talk to him face-to-face, and not

■

> I CONFESSED [TO MY DAD] THAT I HAD NOT
> BEEN A MODEL KID, AND WE BOTH HAD A GOOD
> LAUGH ABOUT THAT UNDERSTATEMENT.

while I was driving. Finally, as I pulled the car into the hotel parking lot, I turned off the engine and I began to pour out my heart to him.

"Dad, I need to communicate something that is very difficult to express. Please know that before I begin, I want to say I deeply love you and honor you." I took a deep breath and I began. "But Dad, I am still hurting over the rejection I felt when you physically punished me as I was growing up. I feel that you crossed the line and as a pastor today, I realize that you had physically abused me."

There was immediate sadness in his eyes. I could almost see that tears were welling up. "After all these years, you are still hurt over what happened when you were a kid?" he inquired incredulously.

"Yes, Dad," I continued. "Dad, you don't have to respond to what I am sharing with you. Just getting this off my chest and expressing something I have wanted to say for a long time is healing enough," I concluded.

My father and I talked for several more minutes. He shared with me how those years were very stressful for him as we strove to survive as immigrants in America. He revealed to me that he had also been abused by his mother, who had a violent temper. Interestingly enough, his father had never hit him.

I confessed that I had not been a model kid, and we both had a good laugh about that understatement. We hugged each other and we expressed our love for one another, and then he went into the hotel.

I drove home elated, but more good news was yet to come. A few minutes after I arrived home, my mother called me from the hotel. She had returned to their room earlier while my father and I had our time alone. Now she was crying on the phone. My mom was crying for me.

"Ché, I am so sorry that you are still feeling pain over something that happened so long ago," she began.

"Mom, I am okay now. I just had to share my heart with Dad and just talking to him has made me feel so much better," I replied.

Then she told me that my father wanted to talk to me, and handed him the phone. I was surprised by that. Immediately, fear came into my heart. My first thought was that Dad was mad at me for exposing him. What happened next is something I will never forget for the rest of my life.

As my father picked up the phone, he said with deep compassion words I had never heard him say or ever expected him to say.

"Son, what I did to you as you were growing up was wrong. Will you ever forgive me?" he queried.

I was stunned. I could hardly believe what I was hearing. I regained my composure enough to respond and assure him that of course I forgave him.

Then he added, "Son, you know how proud I am of you. And I love you very much."

I was so shocked by what I was hearing that I didn't know whether to cry, laugh or shout. "Dad, I love you too," was my only reply. We said good-bye, and as soon as I hung up the phone, I kid you not, I pumped my arm and shouted "Yes!" and then proceeded to dance around the room.

No words can describe the effect this encounter has had in my life. A spirit of rejection was broken off me forever. To this very day, I am seeing and feeling the fruit of this reconciliation. The Scriptures say that God will turn the hearts of the fathers to the children and the children to the father before Christ comes back (see Mal. 4:6). That is exactly what I have experienced and what many others are experiencing during this current move of the Spirit. I believe this is surely a sign of the end-time revival.

That is why I get so perturbed when people criticize this revival as a laughing revival. Yes, God is pouring out His joy; after all, the kingdom of God is "righteousness and peace and joy in the Holy Spirit" (Rom. 14:17, *NKJV*). My experience and my observation is that He is also doing a deep work of convicting us of our sin so we can resolve root issues that have not been addressed and can defile many if left to grow (see Heb. 12:15; 1 John 1:10). That is bringing tremendous freedom and sanctification to many.

Though this newfound liberty and reconciliation with my father was indescribably wonderful, it was only the beginning of a progressively profound change in my personal life that would especially alter my relationship with my wife, Sue.

MAKING IT REAL...PRACTICAL SUGGESTIONS

- Allow the love that God is pouring out through His Spirit to permeate you and every relationship in which you are involved. It is impossible to bring Him into your relationships or to be in His presence and not be changed physically, emotionally and spiritually. What we behold, we become. Make His love your aim.
- Be a learner, and be vulnerable to God's searching in your heart. Realize we all come bearing wounds that need to be healed and that directly affect how we relate to others. One of the greatest blessings of our

faith is the progressive release of Christ's new life in us in exchange for our old lives. Give yourself to the process.

- Attend an Elijah House training, founded by John and Paula Sandford, and/or other credible inner healing workshops.
- Be transparent. Be honest. Confess your faults; repent of any bitter root judgments; and be reconciled to others.

HEART REVIVAL

———————————■———————————

Our marriage was built on a shaky foundation, and I didn't even know it. My wife knew it—but I was deceived. Like a typical husband, my perception of the marriage was totally different from reality.

DOING ALL THE RIGHT THINGS

I believed we had a good marriage because I was doing all the outward things well. Each year, I would set goals for my relationship with Sue, and for the most part, I was good at fulfilling those goals. We had a weekly date night. I brought her flowers. I tried to do something special for her each week. I helped with the dishes and did chores around the house.

We had a family day with the children and we were consistent in our family devotions. We even participated in a marriage accountability group with the other pastoral couples, and each month we shared how we were doing. Once a year we went on a marriage retreat. I was a good provider and bought nice things for Sue. On top of it all, I was a Christian pastor. Outwardly, everything seemed "picture perfect."

I never cheated on Sue; I never went out "drinking with the boys"; and I never hit her. What is more, I felt a deep love for my wife.

Because I "felt" this love and I was doing "all the right things," I thought we had a great marriage. Having been raised as a "performance oriented" person—or one who gets personal validation and sense of worth based on what is accomplished—I equated "doing" with "being" and felt satisfied about the whole scenario.

Performance Oriented

Still, our marriage was lacking some major things. Just as God tells us that man looks on the outward, but He looks on the heart (see 1 Sam. 16:7), so we can do all the right things on the outside and yet be totally selfish on the inside. That is what I was doing in my marriage. Because true love was not coming from my heart, I had a form of godliness without the intimacy and substance that makes a marriage a success.

It did not help that for many years I was part of a church and a charismatic movement that is also performance oriented. This is not to cast an aspersion on any particular movement or church. I thank God for people who are willing to make a difference for the kingdom of God through consistent, decisive and sacrificial action. I believe, however, that most churches have fallen or are subject to a dangerous trap of performance orientation that can seriously hinder the true inner growth of the people in them.

In such an environment, it becomes especially hard for pastors to be real in marriage and family life. Enormous pressure is placed on them to be "examples" and to "have it all together in the home." After all, an elder has to "manage his family well" (1 Tim. 3:4). Little latitude is allowed for variance, and the scrutiny is so great that performing on the surface can become a way of life for pastors.

This affects every person in the pastor's family. Stories abound about pastors' kids or "PKs" who fall from grace because of an inner need to be known and loved for who they are and not for what they do or who their parents are.

Nonetheless, whenever we had our monthly accountability time with the other pastoral couples, the performance competition would begin as we took turns rating our marriages on a scale of 1 to 10. I consistently rated mine around a 7 or an 8. Sue quiet-

■

LIKE A MAGNIFICENT ROSE DYING DAY BY DAY,

MY WIFE ENDURED ME FOR A LONG TIME

UNTIL THE LAST PETAL FELL OFF IN

DISTRAUGHT DESPAIR.

ly nodded or verbally agreed. As the senior pastor's wife and the wife of an Asian male, she felt pressured not to make me look bad.

More than trying not to make me look bad, Sue probably said all the right things from a false loyalty and submission, and a fear of how I might angrily correct her in private. She tried her best to view my monthly assessment as a "positive confession" that might one day become a reality. As this masked charade continued, though, Sue was slowly dying inside. Like a magnificent rose dying day by day, my wife endured me for a long time until the last petal fell off in distraught despair.

EMOTIONAL BREAKDOWN?

It was a summer I will never forget. We were ready to leave for our annual, church family camp in Flagstaff, Arizona. I don't remember what specifically led to the argument, but it wasn't long before "all hell broke loose" in our kitchen. I had never seen Sue so angry in her life.

"I can't stand it anymore! I can't live like this! The way you treat me, the children, and other people is wrong! You don't love me. You're a hypocrite! Stop blaming everything on your choleric personality and Korean culture! Enough!" The words spewed out of her in a deep, angry hurt. I thought at any minute she was going to hit me or scratch out my eyes.

I quickly retaliated by saying, "You call me a hypocrite? Well, look at yourself. You call yourself a Christian, pouring out your venom like that. I pick up nothing but bitterness, and an unsubmissive Jezebel spirit. You're the hypocrite around here!"

Sue was beside herself now. My religious and legalistic response fueled greater desperation. In tears she added, "I'm tired of your judgmental and condemning spirit. You think you are so holy because you can quote the Scriptures, but I am tired of you condemning me with the Bible all the time. You're worse than the Pharisees. I can't take it anymore. I'm trapped, confused and hopeless. I am having a nervous breakdown."

136 | Totally insensitive to her cry, I corrected her for being emotionally manipulative. In my anger, I let her know how I felt. "You are so manipulative with this nervous breakdown threat. Why don't you grow up and repent of this bad attitude? You are really grieving the Spirit, and your root of bitterness is affecting the whole church!"

Her tears continuing to stream down her face, Sue said, "I simply can't take it anymore. You have deeply hurt me over the years, and the children are afraid of you. I can't fake it anymore. I need help! You can go to the conference with the kids; I'm in no position to go. I need psychological help or a counselor or something, because I've lost it!"

Frustrated, exhausted and defeated, she ran into the bedroom sobbing. I felt a mixture of alarm and anger.

Like all couples, we had our share of conflict, but never anything like this. This was the first time she had ever mentioned a nervous breakdown. How dare she blame me for her emotional state! After all, she was the one who was full of bitterness. I reasoned if she would only repent instead of holding on to her hurts, she wouldn't feel this way. All she had to do was act more mature and quit sinning by giving in to these strong, negative emotions.

Besides, how could I go to our church family camp by myself?

People would ask, "Where is Sue?" What would I say? "She couldn't come because she is in the middle of a nervous break-down, but she sends her love." How dare she put me into a situation like this! I looked bad as a husband and a leader. I was mad!

Debating with Sue about coming to camp failed. When I asked for forgiveness, she responded, "Just because you say the right words with your mouth doesn't mean a thing. Your heart hasn't changed, and I don't believe you anymore."

I countered her with Scripture, saying, "We are to forgive 'seventy times seven' every day" (Matt. 18:22, *NKJV*)—causing her to promptly close me off even more. Not only were my comments inappropriate and bad timing, but also a clear example of just how insensitive I had been toward Sue through the years.

The Church Camp Commitment

I left for church camp and took Gabriel and Grace, our two oldest children. Our two youngest, Joy and Mary, remained at home with Sue. I knew I would have to explain to people why my entire family wasn't with me. I told them Joy was sick (which was true) and that Sue stayed back with her, but I knew I had to tell my fellow leaders the real reason my wife was not there.

I disclosed this marital disaster to the two top leaders of our church movement, my fellow brothers in the Lord. I recounted the whole incident to them as accurately as possible. They agreed that I had definitely blown it with Sue, but that she had missed it, too, by displaying her bitterness—just as I had told her.

These men loved me and were committed to helping me in the best way they knew how. As a result, at the end of the conference, one of the brothers and his wife flew to Los Angeles to spend some time with Sue and me to work on the problems in our marriage. They came not only as our friends, but also as our pastors. The problem was serious enough to warrant this special trip.

A Temporary Fix

The best counsel they knew how to offer, however, still did not seem to address the root issues or heart of our problems.

We were asked to repent of our sins, which we sincerely did by confessing our faults and shortcomings, thinking we had repented.

Somehow I could just feel that the real issues and the faulty foundation had not been exposed. We went through the motions, but nothing seemed different. In retrospect, I can see that we were like addicts who try to repent. We mouthed the words, yet there was no inward or permanent change.

The truth of the matter is that none of the four of us had the "tools in our toolbox" at that time to do anything differently or to know what was really needed to effect lasting change.

I have since learned that unless the root issues in our lives are addressed, any change or seeming "repentance" is temporary at best (see Luke 3:9). Just like lopping the top off a dandelion without digging out the roots, the bad fruit of the weed comes right back as soon as it has a chance to grow. Unless the root (or origin) is removed, the destructive process resurfaces, hurting God, self and others.

For the time being, however, things looked good, and the problem appeared to be solved. So our friends flew home and life began to return to normal—or so I thought. That Sunday, I shared in a general way with the congregation about our marital disaster and the help we had received from our friends. We asked the church for forgiveness for letting them down. We told them that we had repented, that we had changed and that things would be different. It would have been better stated to say we *hoped* things *would* change. The plain truth was that nothing had changed. We were more in need of help than ever.

TOUGH LOVE

Our marriage continued to drift. Although I had set new goals to improve our marriage, the fruit didn't change. I continued to live a contradictory and hypocritical life with Sue—filled with fruits of unhealthy criticism, wrongful judgment and, as I would come to discover, emotional and spiritual abuse. I couldn't seem to act any differently.

I was good at fulfilling my external goals, but remained outwardly demanding and emotionally detached from my wife. My accusations and harshness failed to subside. What probably hurt Sue the most was that I kept her love at a distance and refused to allow myself to be emotionally intimate and vulnerable with her.

One major example was the depression I experienced in my ministry in 1993. My wife rightfully wanted to bear my burden with me, but I couldn't let her into my life. Years ago, I heard how one pastor described men as islands and their wives in rowboats trying to find a place to land and settle. I was not only an island, but I had also built a walled fortress, which left no openings to dock!

I just withdrew into my own world, watched an unusual amount of television, and communicated basic information only when necessary. Sue continued to reach out to me, trying to show her care. Yet time after time, I rejected her love, and slowly a part of her died.

The Last Straw
Things came to a head for us again a second time in August 1994.

On one hand, things couldn't have been better. We had just come into the renewal experience, and our church was growing. We had just completed a successful outreach with Roger and Faith Forster from the Ichthus Christian Fellowship in England, leaders who had helped found the International March for Jesus. They had come to Los Angeles accompanied by a team of youth to help us evangelize and to conduct a conference for us. During their visit, Sue and I had our second major blowout.

One night toward the end of the conference, I returned home after the evening meeting with Roger and Faith, who were guests in our home. It was late and we were all tired. Sue left the meeting early to prepare a delicious home-cooked meal for us. Exuding anticipation, she greeted us and invited us all to eat. I declined the invitation because I was exhausted.

Sue could understand the fatigue, but she couldn't accept my response. Instead of thanking her or affirming her efforts or even explaining how tired I was, I simply barked an abrupt, "I'm tired, and I don't want it." After speaking those words, I marched off to bed. That was the last straw. Something inside Sue shut down that night.

Had this been an isolated situation, Sue may have been hurt, but not devastated. This moment culminated 15 years of rejection. My wife responded by doing something I had probably deserved many years sooner. She withdrew emotionally from me. It was a combination of her dying inwardly and choosing to withdraw her emotions from me to protect herself. In her own way, she was showing me "tough love."

Self-Preservation

"Tough love" is a phrase that has been popularized by Dr. James Dobson in his book *Love Must Be Tough*. He essentially advocates that when a spouse repeatedly abuses his or her partner through adultery or physical or emotional abuse, the wife (or husband) needs to demonstrate tough love by separating from the spouse. The purpose of this separation is to shock the spouse into reality, and hopefully lead him or her into repentance and real change. Often this is not a conscious choice of action, but a natural response for self-preservation.

True, I hadn't committed adultery, nor was I physically abusive. I had emotionally and spiritually abused Sue for 15 years, though, and it had taken its toll. She didn't separate from me physically, but she did emotionally.

The amazing thing was she really did not get angry as she had at our first major blowout. In many ways, it would have been easier if she had. She didn't cry. She wasn't mean. In fact, she continued to dutifully serve me as a wife. She did something that was far more painful, though. After years of pouring out her heart to me, laughing with me and being tender toward me, she simply and totally detached herself from me emotionally. It was as if she were emotionally dead.

It didn't take a brain surgeon or a prophet to discern her coolness the next day. I felt as if I had walked into a freezer the next morning when I greeted Sue. Unfortunately, we were still hosting the Forsters and we were too busy to talk.

When we finally did have a chance to talk about it, Sue simply explained that she was tired of being hurt. She felt a need to protect herself from experiencing what she did when she almost had a nervous breakdown. She told me she was not going to make herself emotionally vulnerable anymore and that we needed professional marital counseling.

Brilliant husband that I am, I didn't have a clue what she was talking about. I couldn't believe she would be reacting this way because I refused her dinner. Of course, I didn't realize that the dinner issue was only the tip of the iceberg. The real problem was years and years of rejection.

I looked at the whole incident logically, and felt quite justified that Sue had overreacted and was being unreasonable. I was looking with my intellect and not with my heart, so I had no compassion in my response. I preached that for her to emotionally withdraw from me was a violation of our wedding vows, a sin and inexcusable. I got mad and let her know it. My fellow Pharisees and legalists would have been proud of such a speech of guilt and condemnation.

As time progressed in our marriage, I inwardly became more desperate. Sue performed her perfunctory duties as a wife, albeit without emotions.

A "Bad Season" of Marriage

During the many months that followed, I went through a series of emotional reactions. First, I was extremely mad and I let Sue know it. She simply refused to argue, and said she would walk away from me if she felt condemned or accused. I tried charming her back by speaking words of love and by presenting material gifts. No success! All of the "old stuff" didn't work this time. It was hard accepting the fact that respect and trust had deteriorated so drastically from the foundation of our marriage.

Because I wasn't receiving the results I used to, I decided to be emotionally aloof, thinking two could play this game. Still blinded, though, I could not accept the fact that this was not a game, but a horrible reality. I was convinced the problem was mostly her fault. It was much easier to be in control and continue blaming her for her bitterness than to face the condition of my own heart and any pain I might be carrying or causing.

Because nothing I thought or did changed anything, I finally reasoned this was just a "bad season" in our marriage, but it would soon come to an end. Time would heal everything. Spring always followed winter. This happened to be a bad winter, but it would soon end. I had no idea that winter would last for more than two years.

I often shared with our congregation that renewal has been "the best of times and the worst of times." I never really elaborated on why it was such a difficult time in my life. Of course, the fellow pastors of Harvest Rock Church knew. Because our congregation is an unusual blending of many fellowships coming together, Sue and I had carefully shared what was going on in our marriage with each pastoral couple. We wanted to be honest from day one of Harvest Rock Church.

We took heart that each couple believed in us. Every single one of them expressed continued love and acceptance for Sue and me without judgment or condemnation, and I know this contributed significantly to our healing process.

Each of these pastoral couples also tried to help us in some practical way. They counseled us, corrected us, prophesied over us and prayed for us—but to their discouragement and ours, nothing really significantly or permanently changed. I had asked Sue to forgive me many times, yet she was determined she would not be vulnerable to me again until she felt a godly love where mutual respect and trust could once again safely grow.

Marriage Counseling

Finally, in mutual yet reluctant agreement, we sought a professional marriage counselor. In the past, I had a belief that looked down on professional counselors and Christian psychology, thinking it to be too much like secular psychology. After all, being new creatures in Christ, everything in the past is over and done with—finished! Any other emotional or psychological problem we might ever encounter could be answered straight from the Word of God. It simply never occurred to me that I might need a skilled specialist to help me interpret and implement the Bible's truth in these areas (see Prov. 20:5)!

The renewal helped broaden my outlook—and so did my own personal desperation. I began to move from judgmental and intolerant of Christian counseling to grateful!

I looked forward to those times spent with our marriage counselor. It seemed to be the only time Sue and I could honestly communicate in a safe environment in the presence of an unbiased Christian mediator.

THE TRUTH CAN INDEED HURT, BUT IT
ALWAYS SETS US FREE. THAT IN ITSELF IS
THE DEFINITION OF TRUE LOVE.

Years of pent-up, unresolved issues rooted in both our childhood experiences surfaced, and the thread of our past and our current marriage dilemmas began to make sense. Masks and protective mechanisms coated in religious terms began to dissolve.

Our counselor made a wonderful investment in our lives for which we are eternally grateful—the most significant being the restoration of our personal and mutual identity, self-worth and respect as it originates in Jesus.

Sue and I will forever value this leg on our journey to healing. Yet I must say that it was not the dramatic "end all" I had hoped it would be. Something substantial was still missing in my transformation, and I did not comprehend the missing link.

In my case, Sue's continuing "tough love" worked because there was no way around my facing the reality that something very foundational still needed to change. I now understand her actions to be God's severe, merciful love. The truth can indeed hurt, but it always sets us free. That in itself is the definition of true love.

BAD ROOTS; BAD FRUIT

The renewal has had a profound effect on my life and subsequently on our marriage. In my opinion, its most precious fruit is, and continues to be, renewal from the inside out. In seeing the Father's love for me and in being in a consistent revelation of His love and acceptance, I began to feel safe enough to be honest about my sins and faults.

For years, I had unconsciously put up a front of having my act together, when in reality I was hurting and afraid inside. For most of my Christian life, I suffered a wounded heart and was in major need of inner healing and didn't know it.

Believe me, I was sincere when I confessed before others in times they counseled us about our marriage. I was as sincere as I knew how to be every time I confessed to Sue, though I hadn't really changed. I had not truly repented, or "turned around."

Only when the renewal of the Holy Spirit visited me did revelation come. I began to see that the lack of lasting fruit in my life was related to root problems in childhood that had developed into root sins in my life. Until these roots could be addressed, no lasting change could result.

Time and time again, through confession, I had lopped the top off the dandelion, only to be discouraged when the bad weed surfaced again because the root still lived. This whole new concept of "root issues," or the origin of my behavior and reactions, was a gift of compassion to me from God. It began that night on the floor in Toronto as I went forward for renewal and God showed me the bitter roots I had toward my father.

Healing and Reconciliation

Another major transformation came about during the time God showed me to ask my father for forgiveness when he visited in the fall of 1996. I had no idea how this interaction would affect my relationship with Sue, or how the sin against my father related to the sowing and reaping in my interaction with her.

Yet in the eternal laws of God, that act of obedience was serious and far reaching. Just as He has made every part of our bodies and His body to be interconnected, so the outflow of a change in one area brought tangible change to many others.

■

WHEN WE ARE EMOTIONALLY DAMAGED IN A CLOSE RELATIONSHIP, THE BEST HEALING OF THAT DAMAGE OFTEN COMES THROUGH RECON-CILIATION OF THAT VERY RELATIONSHIP.

When my father asked me at that time to forgive him for abuse, it brought tremendous healing to my heart. Something far greater happened, though—it broke a yoke of oppression over my life. I believe the curse of rejection was broken off me as a blessing from my father was pronounced over me through his repentance and forgiveness.

Then like a floodgate released, and as a husband and rightful spiritual covering over my wife, I automatically released the blessing of love and acceptance over Sue—removing the shame and rejection I had put into her life as well.

God is never mocked. His Word says "you reap what you sow" (see Gal. 6:7). The eternal laws of God exist whether we believe them or not. Determined consequences result for every action. Like the law of gravity, if you jump off a building, you will not fly, but get hurt.

Because I had judged my father and my mother for rejecting me, I had reaped the very thing I had sown. The Bible warns us,

"Do not judge, or you too will be judged. For in the same way you judge others, you will be judged, and with the measure you use, it will be measured to you" (Matt. 7:1,2).

Because I had judged my parents for rejecting me, I had similarly rejected Sue and reaped the same judgment. Though I wasn't physically abusive toward Sue, I had shown the same bitter fruit through emotional and spiritual abuse. Most tragic of all, I withheld from her the very intimacy and emotional vulnerability I had so longed for as a child, and repeatedly rejected her love.

Yet when I had the life-changing conversation with my dad, real root change in my life was set into motion. As he asked me for forgiveness, the bitter root of my judgment toward my father disappeared. The unhealthy cycle of unhealed sin in my life was beginning to be systematically dismantled.

I learned an invaluable principle: When we are emotionally damaged in a close relationship, the best healing of that damage often comes through reconciliation of that very relationship. I not only became reconciled with my father, but that healing, as it so often does, also affected my relationship with my wife, my children, and in an ongoing measure, many other people in my life. In relationships we are wounded, and in relationships we will be healed.

Looking back, I am humbled by how God orchestrated this process of true healing in my life and reconciliation with both my dad and Sue. I never approached my father hoping my marriage would be restored. I never dreamed God would talk to me about bitter roots that night on the floor in Toronto. I could never have assembled such a loving pastoral team to be so supportive and nonjudgmental to help us through the process. I could never manufacture the awesome, life-giving environment of renewal that kept me going in circumstances when I wanted to quit.

God, in His love, initiated it all. He loves us as we are, yet He is committed not to leave us that way! I am so grateful that He placed the desire in my heart to go to my dad. I am forever grateful my father responded in the gracious, humble and repentant way he did so that the process of healing in my life could be fully loosed. God's sovereign hand was in it all.

TAKING UP THE CROSS

Although Sue could see fruit in my life after the reconciliation with my father, it wasn't long before I realized that even though the bad root had been exposed, much work still needed to be done.

The cycle of reaping rejection was broken, but I was still responsible for my sins and the consequences of my choices. I had to repent before God and to Sue. I did not want to merely go through the motions as I had done before. I wanted to know for sure that my heart was transformed. I wanted to know that I could stop rejecting and abusing my wife and others I cared about.

Most of all, I longed to offer Sue the true emotional intimacy and vulnerability deserving of a marriage designed by God.

Fasting and Praying for a Right Heart

A few months after my reconciliation with my dad, I sensed that I needed to enter a time of extended fasting and prayer about this situation. At the same time, our church was hearing the trumpet call sounded by Dr. Bill Bright, and had determined to pray and fast 40 days for worldwide revival.

As my fellow pastors and church members were fasting for revival, I was crying out to God for the revival of my marriage. I believe it is no contradiction of goals. I realized that true revival must always begin with the unevangelized parts of our own human hearts—so I was turning my heart toward home first (see Mal. 4:5,6).

I told the congregation I was fasting for more love in my life. I especially needed more love for Sue and my children. God did not disappoint.

Although I had experienced a major healing experience with my father, I didn't fully understand what had happened until I went away on a personal retreat to continue praying and fasting.

Besides my Bible, I took some important study materials along with me. One item was John and Paula Sandford's book *The Transformation of the Inner Man*, and another, a series of their teaching tapes. For three days I devoured their materials. Much of the terminology and insight in this chapter comes directly from the Sandfords, to whom the Body of Christ and I are ever grateful!

During this time, God began to give me understanding about bitter root judgments, reaping what I had sown and the importance of honoring one's parents. As I fasted, read and listened to what He was saying to me, He began to show me the full significance of what had transpired with my father. Equipped with this fresh and deepening revelation, I further repented before God for the way I had judged my father and my mother and asked Him for a new heart—His heart.

God also began to show me the specific sins I had committed against Sue. He showed me the hard things to which I had been blind: how I had rejected her love; how critical, harsh and judgmental I had been; and the emotional and spiritual abuse. The healing of the root issues that had taken place in my relationship with my parents could now be the same basis for lasting repentance in my attitudes and actions with my wife and children.

Naturally, I wanted to come back and immediately share with Sue what God had revealed to me and repent to her, but I wanted to make sure things were different. I wanted her to see the fruit first before I went to her. She deserved the right to again give her trust and respect if and when she was ready.

Changes continued in my life. After only one year of marriage counseling, Sue told our counselor she thought we could consider bringing closure to our sessions because she noticed significant unhealthy childhood roots had been confronted and resolved, and fruits of grace and hope were coming forth.

To me, that was a decisive sign that lasting transformation of my inner man had begun. I didn't trust myself to discern where I was with Sue because I got it wrong so many times through the years. To hear it from an objective counselor was a new tune!

A week after our last counseling session, my wife and I went out for dinner. Like so many times before, I again asked for forgiveness. Sue and I both sensed this was different, though. I cried as I truly repented.

I had asked for forgiveness before in tears, but nothing had changed. This time, though, Sue could sense the sincerity, and because she had observed a measure of fruit in the previous 12 months, she started to cry as well. She knew that this time my heart was different. She came over to my side of the table and gave me a big hug and a kiss. She totally forgave me. The feeling of warmness and the intimacy was beginning to be restored.

A More Glorious Future

I don't want to kid you and say our marriage is a 10 today. (Are there any 10s this side of glory?) Nor are we totally healed of all our wounds of the past. By the grace of God, however, we are continually working to improve our marriage. Each day we have the choice to put to death on the Cross our temptation to be selfish and revert to old ways, or to prefer one another in Christ.

I can frankly say in many ways our marriage has never been better. For the first time, we are honest about our marriage. For the first time, we have confronted and resolved root issues that were serious and problematic in our marriage.

The major root issue of feeling rejected that had so entangled me in many areas of my life is gone, and I possess a freedom I had never experienced in 24 years of walking with the Lord or 42 years of living. That freedom is translating into a oneness with my wife and children we had never known until the renewal of the Holy Spirit touched our lives.

So we continue to grow daily, and our love for each other continues to deepen. Truly the Lord Jesus Christ has renewed a broken marriage and given us a new start as a family. You see why I am so grateful to God and to this current visitation of His Spirit!

Yet it does not end there. The only way to keep this gift is to freely give it away. This kind of revelation of His love and mercy changes every relationship I have—beginning with God. It changes who I find Him to be, and now, who I see others to be, and what they should and could be as we each strive for "truth in the inner parts" (Ps. 51:6).

This visitation of the Holy Spirit has brought incredible and wonderful changes to my life, my family, Harvest Rock Church and, indeed, throughout the world.

I look back at my life since January 1994, and I have no doubt these years have been the most amazing years of my life. What is more amazing and exciting to me is that this is only preparation for the revival that is going to come to America!

It is worth saying again: This is only *preparation* for the greatest revival and the greatest ingathering of harvest in the history of the Church!

How much more intimacy and transparency does He desire of us, His Bride! How much more wholeness and vulnerability is God's ultimate plan for us as He brings us into oneness with Him! God even describes the mystery of the Church as symbolized by the marriage of the husband and the wife—called together to be "naked,...and were not ashamed" (Gen. 2:25, *NKJV*). It is only appropriate He would begin by addressing the foundations of our closest relationships!

For when the harvest comes, in many ways we will be "reparenting" scores of new converts. We will be "reproducing" after our own kind. If our marriages and family lives are suffering, what kind of example and impact will we have on the harvest?

The Church in America is not yet ready to handle the harvest or His holy and glorious presence when the fullness of revival comes. That is why He is calling us as His Church to be holy as He is holy, and to go ever deeper. For us to be truly holy, we must have true repentance.

True repentance comes when we comprehend the root sins in our lives. In this renewal, the Holy Spirit is doing just that.

He is helping us to understand—and the scales are falling off. God is pouring out incredible grace through this move to become right with Him, and to make things right in our home lives and families.

Responding to this grace makes an incredible difference in the move toward revival. As stated in *Rivers of Revival* by Neil Anderson and Elmer Towns, "The personal and corporate sins of a church will block any future hope of God's blessing or revival. By biblically resolving personal and spiritual conflicts, Christ will be established at the center of people's lives, marriages and ministries of the church. This will allow the Holy Spirit to flow freely through the church and its congregation, thus bringing revival."[1]

This grace is not only available for us to become free in our inner being as never before, but we can also extend that same grace and liberty to others through love. Perhaps the greatest fruit of the whole renewal yet to come is how we can more openly and lovingly reach those who have yet to know Christ.

MAKING IT REAL...PRACTICAL SUGGESTIONS

- Read insightful books such as *The Transformation of the Inner Man* by John and Paula Sandford, *Listening Prayer* by Dave and Linda Olson, and others that can show you the origin of shortcomings in your marriage and relationships with others. Build a library of tapes and videos from these same sources.
- Receive spirit-led Christian counseling for your life and marriage.
- Be held accountable in your marriage.
- Invest time and effort in honing your communication skills with those you love.
- Learn to practice "listening prayer" (Dave and Linda Olson)—or prayer where you specifically ask God to point out your area of pain, the roots of the problem, etc. and then pray through the release. Attend semi-

nars and teachings taught by those skilled in release, such as those sponsored by John and Paula Sandford and Dave and Linda Olson. Share this liberating information with others!

Note

1. Neil T. Anderson and Elmer L. Towns, *Rivers of Revival* (Ventura, Calif.: Regal Books, 1997), p. 24.

THE CYCLE OF REVIVAL:

GOING FROM RENEWAL TO REVIVAL

It has been a privilege to share my wonderful experiences of renewal with you. However, my heart will not be fully released until I also make an appeal. The appeal is that renewal must not be the end; rather, we must go on from renewal to historic revival.

I believe that is what is on God's heart. He gave His Son, not just that a few might be blessed, but that all who believe in Him would receive. He wants a family that spans the globe. Revival is a major way God accomplishes His desire.

On the one hand, revival is something God sovereignly does. On the other hand, I believe we can prepare for the revival. Just as we prepare our homes for a very important guest, so, too, we need to prepare ourselves, our churches and our cities for His arrival. After all, revival is His arrival. So what are we to do, and how are we to prepare for revival?

The best way I know to do this is by capsulizing the themes of this book and integrating them into what I call the "The Cycle of Revival." As we each embrace this cycle, I believe we will move more fully toward a historic revival. I call the process a cycle because we are never intended to arrive at the end of each stage in itself, but, rather, to evolve deeper and deeper in the process.

STAGE I: RECEIVE PERSONAL RENEWAL

It is my conviction that we must continue to experience personal renewal while we pray for, long for and prepare for historic revival. Many people have experienced renewal in places such as Toronto, Canada, and Brownsville Assembly of God in Pensacola, Florida, but have then lost interest in this form of renewal for one reason or another.

A "been there, done that" mentality can hinder us from moving from renewal into revival. Ezekiel 47 describes the water level rising in the Temple and flowing out into the Dead Sea in an ever-increasing measure. Note that Ezekiel did not go into the river, then become disinterested and walk away. Rather, he stayed in the river until the water was so deep that "no one could cross" it (see Ezek. 47:1-5).

We all must hunger for more! As John Arnott says in *The Father's Blessing*: "We are saying, 'Oh, Holy Spirit, we are not satisfied with what we have. It is wonderful. You have increased the anointing. You have increased the power, but oh God, let there be more. Let people be so filled with You that we will see the lame walk, the blind see, the deaf hear, the dead raised and the poor of the world have the gospel preached to them.' That is where the Father wants to take us."[1]

Are we that filled? Are we that hungry? I believe God wants us to experience the refreshing waters of renewal, and then stay in the waters until the water level rises to historic revival. The renewal has brought that kind of a deeper and greater intimacy

with the Father. How can we walk away from something as wonderful as that? The renewal gives forth just such a fresh and mighty
infilling of the Holy Spirit. Why would anyone want to cut it off?

Unfortunately, many do cut it off. I know, however, I must
have that deep drink daily to survive and to be continually
filled with the Holy Spirit (see Eph. 5:18). I believe not one of
us is an exception! That is why I will endeavor to make available personal renewal meetings as often as possible at Harvest
Rock Church, even as our protracted meetings are now entering their fourth year.

In a similar manner, I believe continuing to pursue renewal
also ties in with welcoming the Holy Spirit and being found faithful to welcome Him further as revival comes. When we are faithful in little, God says we will be faithful in much (see Luke 16:10).
That means we must continue to love and embrace the renewal.
Pray as much as you can, and receive as much prayer as you can.
Draw near to God, and He will draw near to you. Receive, and
then give it away as much as you can. If you have not experienced
renewal, then go where you can receive personal prayer and a
new infilling of the Holy Spirit by faith. When we are full of the
Holy Spirit and in love with Jesus, then we are empowered and
desirous to move into the next phase of the cycle.

STAGE II: MAKE WORSHIP
A PRIORITY IN YOUR LIFE

The second stage of the cycle of revival is worship. Ultimately,
revival is the coming of His presence, and His presence comes
as we worship. Worship invites Him in, for the Bible says He
literally "inhabits the praises of Israel [His people]" (Ps. 22:3,
KJV). Likewise, Moses said, "'If your Presence does not go with
us, do not send us up from here'" (Exod. 33:15). Moses so wanted to see God's manifest presence through His glory that he did
not want to go on without it.

It is a gift to be in that place of hunger, for we "will be filled"
(Matt. 5:6). It is an awesome blessing to witness His presence so

155

come in that He literally "takes over," as happened to the priests in 2 Chronicles. In fact, they could not continue their duties, because as they were worshiping God, the manifest presence of God came and filled the Temple (see 2 Chron. 5:2-14).

I must also mention a divine tension at this point. For worship to be true, we must have no other motive than just to be

■

GOD WOULD RATHER HAVE US SEEK HIS FACE (TRUE INTIMACY) THAN SEEK HIS HAND (REVIVAL).

156 with Him. Our goal should not be to "get something from Him." God wants intimacy with us, and He wants us to worship to cultivate that intimacy. Blessedly, when we worship God in Spirit and in truth, the end result is revival!

God would rather have us seek His face (true intimacy) than seek His hand (revival).

This kind of worship is a life of adoration; it is like Mary's as she chose to sit at His feet and be intimate with Him. He wants us to be like Paul, who at the end of His life said, "I consider everything a loss compared to the surpassing greatness of knowing Christ Jesus my Lord, for whose sake I have lost all things" (Phil. 3:8).

The word "knowing" in this context is the kind of deep, unparalleled intimacy a man has with his wife. When we can truly worship Jesus and love Him for who He is, and not for what He can do for us, then we have prepared our hearts for revival.

Because true worship also involves a sacrifice, we must lay down everything on the altar of God. That is why Paul says, "I urge you, brothers, in view of God's mercy, to offer your bodies as living sacrifices, holy and pleasing to God—this is your spiritual act of worship" (Rom. 12:1).

Thus, when we have died to revival as our focus, and when we seek Him for who He is, then our hearts have prepared for revival, and revival is most likely to come. How is this done? Truthfully, I don't know; but I will share how I have prayed.

I simply say, "Father, I want to worship You in Spirit and in truth. I want You for who You are, and not for what You can do, including bringing revival. But I know that my heart is not pure and it is deceitful, so I bring my desires and my agenda for revival to the altar, and I lay it down. If I never see historic revival, but I have more of You, that is more than enough for me. Help me to live this out all the days of my life."

I believe as we maintain this attitude and lifestyle of worship, then God can trust us with revival. If we are longing for revival more than we are longing for Him, however, we have committed the sin of idolatry. So do not strive for revival; just lay it on the altar. Let it die. Instead, be consumed with Him alone. Revival will come before you know it. This principle of dying and letting God resurrect is foundational for not only the rest of this chapter, but also for all God does! You need not strive to make any of the seven preparation points happen. Rather, give it to the Lord and allow Him to do it the way He wants it done and according to His timetable.

157

STAGE III: PURSUE HOLINESS

The Bible says, "Without holiness, no one will see the Lord" (Heb. 12:14).

We will not experience revival without the condition of personal and corporate holiness. Throughout revival history, we observe that holiness was a major condition for revival. Charles Finney (an American evangelist during the Second Great Awakening, 1792-1875) said that revival is nothing more than a new beginning of obedience to God. Biblically, we notice how repentance precedes revival in passages such as 2 Chronicles 7:14; Joel 2:12-32; Acts 2:38; and Acts 3:19.

Please allow me to explain what I mean by being "holy."

Positionally, all believers are holy. The Bible says we are "a holy nation" (1 Pet. 2:9). However, God wants us to be holy in practice. To be holy, then, means to be set apart and to cease practicing "the sin that so easily entangles" us (Heb. 12:1).

We cannot do this in our own strength. Be honest with God, and tell Him you cannot overcome any sin apart from His grace. By grace you were saved, and by grace you will be saved (see Eph. 2:8). What we can do is ask God to help us be aware of our sins. Then we must repent of every sin He shows us. Repentance is then hating and forsaking our sins. It is laying our sins on the altar and killing them. It is dying to those sins on the Cross daily.

When I repent, I may say something like, "Father, I have this anger toward my brother. I cannot change myself, but I come to You to receive grace and mercy by faith. I repent of the sin of anger and I ask for Your forgiveness. I come to Your cross and I ask You to help me crucify this anger on the cross. By faith, I receive Your forgiveness and deliverance in Jesus' name."

I think this is what it means to take up the Cross daily, and what it means to confess your sins. It is then He will forgive you and deliver you from your sin (see 1 John 1:9).

By doing this with every sin, and every time we sin, we learn to pray without ceasing and practice the presence of the Holy Spirit. I believe this continuous process is what it means to be thoroughly right with God and to practice holiness.

Sometimes, however, we are not aware of our sins. It is then we need others to help us, especially those who have the gift of counseling. I highly recommend Elijah House Ministries founded by John and Paula Sandford. As I shared in the last two chapters, their teachings and ministry have changed my life, that of my family and that of my church.

Another vital way to continue to be transformed into His holy likeness is through receiving continued prayer for personal renewal. Many have experienced a deeper sanctifying work of the Holy Spirit through the previously mentioned renewal meetings in places such as Toronto and Pasadena. Surely, there is no higher form of freedom than that gained by the Master's skillful touch—often in areas where we did not even know we had missed the mark.

Finally, I believe a crucial factor in holiness before the Lord is that we must enter into identificational prayer. This is the kind of repentance we notice with Daniel (see Dan. 9) and Nehemiah (see Neh. 2). It is where we identify with the sins of the Church, our city and our nation. God dealt with Israel as "one man," and has always called upon a "people," so both personal and corporate repentance is crucial preparation for historic revival.

STAGE IV: INTERCEDE FOR THE LOST

I once heard someone say that historical revival has never taken place without united prayer being first on the agenda. We all know that prayer is an indispensable condition for revival. How shall we pray? Paul gives the answer by saying, "Pray in the Spirit on all occasions with all kinds of prayers and requests" (Eph. 6:18).

Let me suggest three levels of prayer.

First, every believer should be praying for revival and for the lost (see 1 Tim. 2:1ff.). One effective and practical way is by praying for your *oikos*. *Oikos* is the Greek word meaning household. The household consists of friends and relatives who live nearby. For example, when Peter preached to the household *(oikos)* of Cornelius, we read he "had called together his relatives and close friends" (Acts 10:24). Those people are the ones who came to Christ that day.

I have been praying for my *oikos* for years, and I have seen every one of my family members and my relatives in the United States come to know Christ. Your *oikos* may include "prayer-walking" your neighborhood and crying out for souls. I believe it was J. Oswald Sanders, the great New Zealand Christian leader, who said, "It is doubtful that any soul is saved apart from the believing prayer of some saint."

Second, I would encourage you to pray in agreement with others regularly. The Bible says, "'If two of you on earth agree about anything you ask for, it will be done for you by my Father in heaven'" (Matt. 18:19). There is power in agreement. Pray with others, either in a small group or in a corporate prayer meeting.

Finally, I believe it is important for pastors to pray together in their city.

Pastors and apostolic leaders are the gatekeepers and the highest authority in the city. It is crucial they meet regularly for

■

> TWO CONDITIONS ARE NECESSARY
>
> FOR REVIVAL: PRAYER AND UNITY
>
> (CHARLES FINNEY).

prayer. One of the most powerful things we are doing in Los Angeles is for two to three hundred pastors to come together for prayer three to four times a year through the umbrella organization Love L.A., founded by Pastor Jack Hayford. Prayer groups for pastors are being formed across the country. I want to encourage every pastor reading this to be involved with prayer in your city.

As Ed Silvoso says in *That None Should Perish*, "Cities are central to God's redemptive strategy. The Great Commission begins with a city—Jerusalem—and culminates when another city—the New Jerusalem—becomes God's eternal dwelling with His people. In order to fulfill the Great Commission, we must reach every city on earth with the gospel."[2] Unified prayer is the first step.

STAGE V: PURSUE UNITY

Charles Finney, the famed American revivalist, said in *Revival Lectures* that basically two conditions are necessary for revival:

prayer and unity.[3] He was talking about the unity of the Church. D. L. Moody, famed nineteenth-century urban revivalist, said in *Secret Power*, "I never yet have known the Spirit of God to work where the Lord's people were divided."[4]

I believe there are several levels of unity.

First, we should be reconciled to others—period. An abundance of Bible verses speak of forgiveness and reconciliation. This point needs no belaboring. We must just do it! We need to be reconciled—brothers to brothers, fathers to sons, and husbands to wives—to be at peace with all men "as far as it depends on you" (Rom. 12:18).

Second, unity and love must be apparent within a local church. God is purging the Church of slander, gossip and criticism. He is serious about this sin. If we are not a part of the problem or the solution to it, it is not our place to get involved. We must each be careful about not only what we speak, but also what we hear. I strongly want to encourage people not to speak evil of their pastors or the church leadership. Don't divide the Body and bring a reproach on him "for whom Christ died" (Rom. 14:15; see also 1 Cor. 8:11). Do not bring an accusation against an elder unless you have "two or three witnesses" (1 Tim. 5:19). This is a serious hour in which God is dealing with the Church as a whole, and Achan's sin will be found out and affect the whole camp (see Josh. 7:1). When one suffers, all will suffer (see 1 Cor. 12:26), so we must approach what we say and believe about others with great soberness, humility and forgiveness.

Third, unity must exist among believers within the citywide Church. As I shared how the Lord dealt with me in Argentina, so we need to embrace God's perspective. There is only one Church, regardless of the denominational lines. We need to repent of any arrogance that we are better than other churches or kinds of people and we need to repent of any sectarianism or exclusivism.

Finally, I believe the Lord is requiring us to be reconciled among the various races. I heard Billy Graham say the number one sin in the Body of Christ is the sin of racism. We need to repent and be reconciled. We need to continue to break down the strongholds of racism by coming in the opposite spirit of love and unity. How about planning a joint service with a church of another color? How about inviting a person of another culture to speak at your church or conference? How would you feel if your son or daughter came home and told you he or she wanted to marry a godly person, but the person was of another color? This is where the rubber meets the road, and we need to ask God to help us overcome racism in our hearts.

STAGE VI: PREPARE THE NETS

We need to prepare the nets in the local church and in the Body of Christ at large. What if God did give us a great harvest overnight? What would we do with all those who come in? Are our nets prepared? Could we handle the fish as well as "clean" and care for them?

I was saved during the Jesus Movement, and I observed thousands do the same. Yet many of them fell away because churches were not ready to handle the harvest. We need churches that can incorporate, care, disciple and release laborers into the harvest. It takes a process to help do that. The Holy Spirit will lead you.

Train for the Harvest

You may wish to consider one way He is leading Harvest Rock Church to conserve the harvest. We have established the Alpha Course, a several-week training and fellowship outreach, not only to evangelize the lost, but also to lay a solid foundation in the faith for new believers. When participants finish the course, we encourage them to do two things: first, be involved in our cell groups; second, attend our new-members class. By attending and completing the new-members class, we offer a solid way to become committed not only to Jesus, but also to the church.

In our new-members seminar, we emphasize the importance of getting involved in a cell group or a small, home group. I believe the emphasis on cell groups by people such as

Larry Stockstill, Yonggi Cho and Lawrence Kong is what the Holy Spirit is saying to the Church today. The cell structure is the best way to retain the harvest.

We are also establishing a one-session class for those who are members to help them become involved in a ministry within the church. Finally, we offer a one-year School of Ministry for those who are serious about vocational ministry as a church planter or a missionary.

Through this series of outreaches, a new convert can potentially come to Christ, become incorporated in the church life through small groups and ministry involvement and, if appropriate, be trained to enter vocational ministry.

I am not so much advocating our model (if it does help, wonderful), but, rather, a diligent and progressive system to process the harvest. It must encompass every level of the local church, and also be felt throughout.

Yet the most important element of the system is that we bring people into a loving community of believers. People are looking for a sense of belonging. Consider the gang problems among the youth. These kids believe they don't belong in their homes or in society. Most have no personal family life. Therefore, we need to be that family for those who come to Christ. The church is an army, but it is first a family. We must demonstrate the love and care and sense of family to effectively receive the harvest.

Network with Other Churches

The second level of preparing the nets for the harvest is through networking with other churches in your city. We need to have such unity and love that if a new convert could be better served in another church, we won't hesitate to recommend or send that person there. In the same way, if people leave to attend another church, we need to bless and release them instead of condemning or trying to hold on to them.

Ted Haggard describes it like this in his book *Primary Purpose*: "Our primary purpose does not require every church to reach every person. It would be impossible. God would not allow it because it would violate his establishment of the body. Instead God requires us to reach a specific flavor in the body of Christ and our co-worker to reach still another group. Through the strength we draw from our different flavors, we can communicate to the various people within our communities."[5]

Remember, there is only one Church in the city. As long as people are not joining a cult, we should bless them and give them the ultimate right to hear from Jesus about where to be planted. I believe we will yet see such a large harvest that all the church buildings in a given city will not be able to hold the harvest, even by scheduling multiple services! I believe it will be just like Peter calling for the other boats (churches) to help him pull in the net. So let us do it with joy together!

164

Plant New Churches

On another level, we need to plant as many new churches as possible. Peter Wagner has said church planting is the most effective way of evangelizing the lost.[6] That is why we have formed the apostolic network called Harvest International Ministries. We want to fulfill the Great Commission by planting as many churches as possible before the Lord comes.

Unite Efforts

Finally, let me encourage apostolic networks, ministries and denominations to each pull together and unite their efforts to reach and receive the harvest. The Bible says we have exponential strength to the tenth power greater each time we do (see Deut. 32:30)!

STAGE VII: BE COMMITTED TO EVANGELISM AND MISSIONS

Regardless of whether we are in a revival mode or not, we must evangelize. We have a mandate from our Lord that gives us no options (see Mark 16:15). We can be wrongly passive in our thinking by believing the harvest will come in and we simply have to receive.

On the contrary, any farmer will tell you that when it is harvest time, more work is done than any other time of the year. Jesus said, "occupy till I come" (Luke 19:13, *KJV*). That means we must continue to do the works of Jesus while it is still day. Night comes "when no one can work" (John 9:4). The truth is that revival comes as we are obedient to God. Charles Finney said revival is nothing more than a new beginning of obedience to God; in the same way we make great headway toward revival as we obey the Great Commission.

As I mentioned before, I love any method of evangelism, as long as it is effective. Prayer evangelism advocated by Ed Silvoso is a tremendous way to start. "Seeker sensitive" churches have also been very effective. It has been my observation that it is hard for charismatic churches to make the transition to a seeker-sensitive format. For those who are charismatic and who belong to renewal-oriented churches, I would highly recommend you look into the Alpha Course (see the bibliography at the end of this book for more information).

The Alpha Course was started by a charismatic, renewal-oriented church in England—Holy Trinity Church of Brompton. Alpha combines friendship evangelism and proclamation evangelism with power evangelism. Alpha is a "seeker friendly" Bible study taught on a midweek night. It begins with dinner and a fun time of fellowship, moves forward into excellent video teaching and ends with small-group discussion. At the end of 7 weeks, people are invited to attend a retreat where they are prayed for to receive the infilling of the Holy Spirit. After 10 weeks, they are taught about commitment to a local church and are encouraged to attend a small group such as a cell group.

Alpha is wonderful because it is totally locally church based, and fully prepared and presented in video format so you do not have to "recreate the wheel." Yet it allows for plenty of room for your church's individual expression to emerge in the small-group discussions, skits and fellowship meals that are a part of the plan.

The bottom line in choosing any successful means of evangelism is to be full of the Holy Spirit. Jesus said, "'You will receive power when the Holy Spirit comes on you; and you will be my witnesses'" (Acts 1:8). We need to be so full of God that evangelism naturally overflows into all we say and do. That leads us back to the first step of this cycle, personal renewal. By continuing this cycle of renewal, worship, holiness, prayer, unity, preparation and evangelism, I believe we will come into historic revival and a great worldwide harvest. More important, each day we move one step closer to seeing His glorious face!

May the renewal of the Holy Spirit continue to transform your life and the lives of those around you...for indeed, the best is yet to come!

Notes

1. John Arnott, *The Father's Blessing* (Lake Mary, Fla.: Creation House, 1995), p. 233.
2. Ed Silvoso, *That None Should Perish* (Ventura, Calif.: Regal Books, 1994), p. 21.
3. Charles Finney, *Revival Lectures* (Grand Rapids: Fleming H. Revell, n.d.), p. 349.
4. Dwight L. Moody, *Secret Power* (Ventura, Calif.: Regal Books, 1987), p. 124.
5. Ted Haggard, *Primary Purpose* (Lake Mary, Fla.: Creation House, 1995), p. 93.
6. C. Peter Wagner, *Church Planting for a Great Harvest* (Ventura, Calif.: Regal Books, 1990).

SELECTED
BIBLIOGRAPHY

Anderson, Neil T., and Elmer L. Towns. *Rivers of Revival*. Ventura, Calif.: Regal Books, 1997.

Arnott, John. *The Father's Blessing*. Lake Mary, Fla.: Creation House, 1995.

Bright, Bill. *The Coming Revival*. Orlando, Fla.: NewLife Publications, 1995.

Brown, Michael L. *Let No One Deceive You*. Shippensburg, Pa.: Revival Press, 1997.

Bryant, David. *The Hope at Hand*. Grand Rapids: Baker Books, 1995.

Campbell, Wesley. *Welcoming a Visitation of the Holy Spirit*. Lake Mary, Fla.: Creation House, 1996.

Cannistraci, David. *Apostles and the Emerging Apostolic Movement*. Ventura, Calif.: Regal Books, 1996.

Chevreau, Guy. *Catch the Fire*. London, England: Marshall Pickering, 1994.

Cooke, Graham. *Developing Your Prophetic Gifting*. Kent, England: Sovereign World International, 1994.

Dawson, John. *Taking Our Cities for God*. Lake Mary, Fla.: Creation House, 1989.

Finney, Charles. *Revival Lectures*. Grand Rapids: Fleming H. Revell Company. n.d.

Goll, Jim. *The Lost Art of Intercession*. Shippensburg, Pa.: Revival Press, Destiny Image Publishers, 1997.

Haggard, Ted. *Primary Purpose*. Lake Mary, Fla.: Creation House, 1995.

Hamon, Bill. *Prophets and Personal Prophecy.* Shippensburg, Pa.: Destiny Image Publishers, 1987.

Jacobs, Cindy. *The Voice of God.* Ventura, Calif.: Regal Books, 1995.

Joyner, Rick. *The Final Quest.* New Kensington, Pa.: Whitaker House, 1996.

Moody, Dwight L. *Secret Power.* Ventura, Calif.: Regal Books, 1987.

Olson, Dave and Linda. *Listening Prayer.* El Cajon, Calif.: Listening Prayer Ministries, 1996.

Otis Jr., George. *The Twilight Labyrinth.* Grand Rapids: Chosen Books, 1997.

Pratney, Winkie. *Revival: Its Principles and Personalities.* Lafayette, La.: Huntington House, 1994.

Randolph, Larry. *User Friendly Prophecy.* Shippensburg, Pa.: Destiny Image Publishers, 1998.

Sandford, John and Paula. *The Elijah Task.* Tulsa, Okla.: Victory House, Inc., 1977.

——. *The Transformation of the Inner Man.* Tulsa, Okla.: Victory House, Inc., 1982.

Sheets, Dutch. *Intercessory Prayer.* Ventura, Calif.: Regal Books, 1996.

Silvoso, Ed. *That None Should Perish.* Ventura, Calif.: Regal Books, 1994.

Sjogren, Steve. *Conspiracy of Kindness.* Ann Arbor, Mich.: Vine Books, Servant Publications, 1993.

Smith, Alice. *Beyond the Veil.* Ventura, Calif.: Renew Books, 1997.

Wagner, C. Peter. *Church Planting for a Great Harvest.* Ventura, Calif.: Regal Books, 1990.

——. *How to Have a Healing Ministry in Any Church.* Ventura, Calif.: Regal Books, 1988.

——. *Spiritual Power and Church Growth.* Lake Mary, Fla.: Strang Communications, 1986.

——. *The Third Wave of the Holy Spirit.* Ann Arbor, Mich.: Vine Books, Servant Publications, 1988.

Wimber, John and Kevin Springer. *Power Evangelism.* San Francisco: HarperSanFrancisco, 1986; 2nd revised and expanded edition, 1992.

Other Resources
Magazine:
Spread the Fire Anniversary Issue 4, no. 1 (January 1998). Toronto Airport Christian Fellowship, Toronto, Ontario, Canada.

Alpha Course:
For more information contact:
109 E. 50th St.
New York, NY 10022
Phone: 212-378-0292
E-mail: alphana@aol.com

Conferences

Strategic conferences held at Mott Auditorium in Pasadena several times each year seek to **train, equip and fill the Body of Christ** with the Lord's presence, passion and destiny. We are blessed to host the finest leaders and visionaries of the many streams of Christ's Body in this hour.

Registration fees are kept as low as possible to enable the most people to partake from the bounty God is providing.

Missions Conferences: Whether you are a seasoned missionary or fledgling, ardent supporter or intercessor, or solidly among the ranks of God's soldiers today, our annual mission conference will take you further and higher in the purposes of God and helping reach the global harvest. Key world leaders such as John Dawson, Cindy Jacobs, Ralph Winter, Ralph Mahoney and more join us for these prayerfully themed life-changing gatherings.

Catch the Fire Conferences: Join anointed ministers such as John Arnott from Toronto, Rick Joyner, Paul Caine, Frank Demazio, Gerald Coates, Mike Bickle, Tommy Tenney and more for these glorious, Spirit-led convocations. Leave filled with the glory, wisdom and power needed to rise and do that to which God has called you.

Youth and Special Focus Conferences: Additional conferences held at Mott throughout the year include Rock the Nations Youth conferences and specially focused events such as our family conference, Healing the Wounded Heart conference, and more.

To be added to our conference and special speaker's events mailing list, please call 626-794-1199 or write to Harvest Rock Church 1539 E. Howard St., Pasadena, CA 91104 or add your information online at our Web site, www. grmi.org/churches/harvestrock.

Learn to Fight on Your Knees

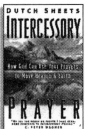